Tra
RHINE
VALLEY
GERMANY

Unforgettable Memories Awaits!

Daniel K. Grinder

COPYRIGHT NOTICE

This publication is copyright protected. This is only for personal use. No part of this publication may be, including but not limited to, reproduced, in any form or medium, stored in a data retrieval system or transmitted by or through any means, without prior written permission from the Author / Publisher.

Legal action will be pursued if this is breached.

DISCLAIMER

Please note that the information contained within this document is for educational purposes only. The information contained herein has been obtained from sources believed to be reliable at the time of publication. The opinions expressed herein are subject to change without notice.

Readers acknowledge that the Author / Publisher is not engaging in rendering legal, financial or professional advice. The Publisher / Author disclaims all warranties as to the accuracy, completeness, or adequacy of such information.

The Publisher assumes no liability for errors, omissions, or inadequacies in the information contained herein or from the interpretations thereof. The publisher / Author specifically disclaims any liability from the use or application of the information contained herein or from the interpretations thereof.

TABLE OF CONTENTS

Copyright Notice 3
Disclaimer 4
TABLE OF CONTENTS 5
    INTRODUCTION 13

Welcome to Rhine Valley, Germany! 13
    About the Travel Guide 14
    Why Rhine Valley, Germany? 15
    How to Use This Guide 17
    CHAPTER 1 21

Introduction 21
    Overview of the Rhine Valley 21
    Historical and Cultural Significance 24
    What to Expect During Your Visit 26
    CHAPTER 2 30

Top Tourist Attractions 30
    Lorelei Rock 31

- Heidelberg Castle. 32
- Marksburg Castle. 34
- Rhine Gorge. 36
- Bacharach 38
- Koblenz Deutsches Eck. 40
- Rüdesheim am Rhein. 42
- Boppard. 44
- Burg Eltz. 47
- Mainz Cathedral. 49
- CHAPTER 3 52

Overview of Accommodation Options. 52
- Luxury Resorts. 53
- Budget-Friendly Hotels 55
- Boutique Guesthouses. 57
- Unique Stays 60
- Most Recommended Accommodation 62
- Selecting the Right Accommodation for You 64
- Booking Tips & Tricks. 65
- CHAPTER 4 68

Itinerary for Different Travelers 68
- Weekend Getaway. 69

- Cultural Immersion 71
- Outdoor Adventure 75
- Family-Friendly Travel 78
- Budget Travel 81
- Solo Traveler's Guide 85
- Romantic getaways 88
- CHAPTER 5 92

How To Get There 92
- By Air 93
- By Train 95
- By Car 97
- By Boat 99
- CHAPTER 6 102

The Best Time to Visit 102
- Seasonal Overview 103
- Festivals & Events 106
- Weather Considerations 108
- CHAPTER 7 111

Duration of Stay 111
- Recommended length of stay 112

Recommended Itineraries for Various Lengths....................115

CHAPTER 8 120

Practical Things. 120

Currency and Payment..121

Local Customs and Etiquette 122

Language & Communication 124

Health & Safety..126

CHAPTER 9 128

Transportation in the Rhine Valley 128

Public Transportation. 129

Car Rental 132

Cycling and Walking 134

Taxis and Ridesharing..135

CHAPTER 10 137

Dining and Cuisine 137

Traditional Rhine Valley Dishes...138

Recommended Restaurants and Cafés 140

Local Food Markets. 142

CHAPTER 11 145

Shopping..145

Souvenirs & Gifts 146

Local Markets and Shops 148

Shopping Districts 150

CHAPTER 12 153

Nightlife & Entertainment 153

Bars and clubs. 154

Live Music & Performances 156

Cultural Activities and Festivals 158

CHAPTER 13 161

Outdoor Activities. 161

Hiking Trails. 162

river cruises..164

Cycle Routes...166

Natural Reserves and Parks 169

CHAPTER 14 172

Family-Friendly Activities. 172

Attractions for Children 173

Family-Friendly Restaurants..176

Educational and Interactive Experiences. 180

CHAPTER 15 187

-8-

Cultural Experiences..187
    Museums & Galleries 188
    Historic Sites 192
    Local Traditions and Festivals..............................195
    CHAPTER 16 199

Health and Wellness 199
    Spa and Wellness Centers 200
    Fitness and Recreation..202
    Medical Service 204
    CHAPTER 17 207

Safety & Security 207
    Emergency Services..208
    Travel Safety Tips. 211
    Local Laws and Regulations. 213
    CHAPTER 18 217

What to Do and Not to Do. 217
    Do's 218
    DON'TS 220
    Locale Etiquette 222
    CHAPTER 19 225

Tips for First-Time Visitors. 225
   Common Pitfalls To Avoid 226
   Essential Travel Tips 228
   Make the Most of Your Trip 230
   CHAPTER 20 234

Sustainable Travel. 234
   Eco-Friendly Practices. 235
   Supporting Local Businesses 238
   Responsible Tourism 240
   CHAPTER 21 244

Local Experiences and Hidden Gems. 244
   Off-Beaten-Path Attractions 245
   Unique Local Experiences 248
   Suggested Local Guides and Tours 250
   CHAPTER 22 253

Appendix 253
   Emergency Contacts 254
   Maps and Navigational Tools 256
   Additional Reading and References 258
   Useful Local Phrases 260

Addresses and Locations of Popular Accommodation 262

Addresses and Locations of Popular Restaurants and Cafés 265

Addresses and Locations of Popular Bars and Clubs 269

Addresses and Locations of Top Attractions........................272

Addresses and Locations of Bookshops...............................275

Addresses and Locations of Top Clinics, Hospitals, and Pharmacies..279

Addresses and Locations of UNESCO World Heritage Sites .283

INTRODUCTION

WELCOME TO RHINE VALLEY, GERMANY!

Welcome to the Rhine Valley, a beautiful region in Germany known for its spectacular scenery, rich history, and attractive villages. The Rhine Valley, nestled between rolling hills and stately castles, provides a unique combination of natural beauty and cultural legacy. From the famed Lorelei Rock to the ancient villages of Bacharach and Rüdesheim, this region offers a wealth of experiences waiting to be discovered.

As you travel through the Rhine Valley, you'll be enveloped in a scenery that appears to have stepped directly out of a fairy tale. The river runs through vineyards, historic castles, and tiny villages, creating a canvas that is both fascinating and diverse. The Rhine Valley offers an amazing experience, whether you're exploring ancient buildings, indulging in local wines, or simply admiring the tranquil beauty of the Rhine.

About the Travel Guide

Comprehensive coverage

This trip guide is intended to be your ideal companion when touring the Rhine Valley. It is designed with both first-time tourists and seasoned travelers in mind, providing a wealth of information to help you make the most of your stay. We've included thorough descriptions of prominent attractions, practical information, and insider tips to make your trip pleasurable and stress-free.

You'll discover extensive coverage of the Rhine Valley's main attractions, from the lively metropolis of Koblenz and Mainz to the quiet beauty of the vineyards and castles. Each chapter contains interesting insights, recommended activities, and practical guidance to help you easily traverse the region.

Practical Tips

Our guide is more than simply a list of sites; it also includes useful recommendations to help you organize your vacation. We go over everything from how to go to the Rhine Valley and when is the ideal time to visit, to transportation alternatives and local customs. Whether you're seeking for opulent lodgings or low-cost choices, our guide has thorough recommendations to fit all tastes and budgets.

Itineraries for All Types of Travelers

To help planning your trip easier, we've provided a range of itineraries geared toward different interests and travel preferences. Whether you're a history buff, a nature lover, or a foodie, you'll discover suggested itineraries that showcase the Rhine Valley's top attractions. Each itinerary is designed to help you explore the region in a way that is tailored to your own interests and time restrictions.

Local insights

One of this guide's features is its emphasis on local knowledge. We've delved into the wisdom of residents and professionals to provide ideas and insights that go beyond the conventional tourist experience. From hidden jewels to must-try local cuisine, you'll get a taste of the Rhine Valley from a native's viewpoint.

Why Rhine Valley, Germany?

Rich History and Culture

The Rhine Valley is rich in history and culture, making it an intriguing destination for history buffs. The region is littered with castles that have weathered the test of time, each with a unique narrative to tell. Heidelberg Castle, with its breathtaking vistas and historical significance, is just one of the numerous historical sites waiting to be discovered. Furthermore, the Rhine Valley is home to attractive villages with well-preserved medieval architecture, providing a look into history.

Scenic Beauty

The natural splendor of the Rhine Valley is really breathtaking. The river is the focal point, running through a setting of rich vineyards, undulating hills, and towering cliffs. The Rhine Gorge, a UNESCO World Heritage site, is known for its scenic vistas and plethora of castles located on the slopes. The shifting seasons provide diverse viewpoints on the terrain, ranging from vivid spring blooms to golden fall foliage.

Wine and Gastronomy

The Rhine Valley is a wine lover's heaven. The region is known for its vineyards, which produce some of Germany's best wines. A visit to the Rhine Valley allows you to try beautiful Rieslings and other local varietals while seeing the picturesque vineyard settings. Local food compliments the wine nicely, with traditional meals and regional delicacies that highlight the area's rich tastes.

Vibrant festivals and events

The Rhine Valley is particularly renowned for its lively festivals and festivities. Throughout the year, you may attend a variety of festivals that reflect the region's culture and customs. The Rhine Valley hosts a variety of events, from wine festivals to medieval fairs. These events offer a unique opportunity to immerse oneself in local culture while also enjoying the festive atmosphere.

Accessibility and Convenience

One of the most significant advantages of the Rhine Valley is its accessibility. It is located in western Germany and is well connected by major transit lines, making it easily accessible from all across Europe. The region has a variety of hotel alternatives, from opulent resorts to lovely guesthouses, so you may choose a location that meets your needs and interests. Furthermore, the well-developed public transit system allows you to explore the region without the need for a car.

How to Use This Guide

Plan Your Itinerary

Begin by utilizing this guidance to create an itinerary depending on your interests and the length of your visit. Each chapter has thorough information on sites, lodgings, and activities, allowing you to design a tailored vacation itinerary. We recommend reading the sections on prominent tourist sites and itineraries to get a feel for what the Rhine Valley has to offer.

Navigating The Regions

As you tour the Rhine Valley, use the sections on transportation and practical tips to help you traverse the area. Our guide offers advice for getting around, whether you're taking public transportation, renting a car, or exploring on foot. This information will assist you in easily transitioning from one location to another and making the most of your stay in the region.

Making the most of local insights

Use the local insights offered in this guide to improve your experience. Look for recommendations on hidden gems, local eating alternatives, and one-of-a-kind experiences that other travel books may overlook. Engaging with the local culture and community will enhance your vacation and provide unique experiences.

Staying informed

Keep the practical advice section available for information about currencies, local traditions, and emergency numbers. This will guarantee that you are fully prepared for any situations that may happen throughout your vacation. Furthermore, the appendix at the conclusion of the guide has essential addresses, maps, and other resources to keep you organized and informed during your travel.

Enjoying your stay

Finally, keep in mind that this guide is intended to improve your experience, not to dictate every aspect of your trip. Feel free to explore impulsively and delight in the unexpected discoveries that make travel so pleasant. Use the guide as a resource to help you plan your vacation, and let the Rhine Valley's charm and beauty unfold while you explore this magnificent region.

CHAPTER 1

INTRODUCTION

Overview of the Rhine Valley

The Rhine Valley is a beautiful region in western Germany that runs along the Rhine River from the Swiss border to the city of Köln. This region is renowned for its breathtaking scenery, beautiful towns, and a rich tapestry of history and culture. The Rhine River, one of Europe's most significant waterways, is the valley's lifeblood, flowing through a range of landscapes, from mild vineyards to dramatic cliffs and charming cities.

Natural beauty

The Rhine Valley is known for its stunning natural beauty. The river is a key element, with its waters reflecting the changing hues of the seasons. On each side of the river, you'll discover undulating hills covered with vineyards, lush forests, and sheer cliffs with beautiful vistas. The Rhine Gorge, commonly known as the Upper Middle Rhine Valley, is renowned for its beautiful beauty. This UNESCO World Heritage site is well-known for its spectacular vistas and countless castles dotting the slopes, each with a unique narrative to tell.

Wine Country

The region is one of Germany's most well-known wine-producing districts. The vineyards around the Rhine River are well-known for producing superb wines, notably Rieslings. The Rhine Valley's microclimate and soil characteristics provide an ideal setting for viticulture, making it a favorite destination for wine connoisseurs. Visitors may participate in wine excursions, tastings, and festivals that highlight the local wine culture.

Charming towns.

The Rhine Valley is filled with quaint towns and villages that appear to have sprouted from a fairy tale. Bacharach, Rüdesheim, and Boppard have attractive streets, old buildings, and a pleasant attitude. These towns frequently include classic half-timbered buildings, cobblestone streets, and bustling marketplaces where you may sample the region's culture and friendliness.

Recreational Opportunities

For individuals who prefer outdoor sports, the Rhine Valley offers several chances for hiking, cycling, and river cruises. The visual grandeur of the Rhine may be fully appreciated by taking one of the many hiking routes that provide panoramic views of the river and its surroundings. Cycling lanes along the river are well-maintained and offer a relaxing opportunity to explore the valley. Additionally, river cruises provide a relaxing and scenic option to view the countryside from the water.

Historical and Cultural Significance

The Rhine Valley has a rich historical and cultural legacy dating back millennia. Its importance is evident in the various historical landmarks, architectural marvels, and cultural traditions that have formed the area.

Historical importance

The Rhine River has been an important trading route since Roman times. Because of its strategic location, the valley has long been a hub for commercial and military activity. Roman remains, such as vestiges of walls and towns, may still be seen along the river, providing a look into history.

Throughout the Middle Ages, the Rhine Valley was a center of power and influence. The erection of multiple castles and strongholds along the river was a strategic and symbolic act. These castles were erected to protect regions and gain control of trade routes. Many of these ancient castles, like Marksburg Castle and Eltz Castle, have been scrupulously conserved and are available to the public, affording an intriguing glimpse into the region's feudal history.

Cultural Heritage

The Rhine Valley is also renowned for its rich cultural heritage. The region has been influenced by a variety of cultures, including Roman, Frankish, medieval, and contemporary. The area's architecture, festivals, and culinary traditions all reflect its ethnic richness.

The valley is known for its contributions to literature and music. The romanticism of the Rhine Valley influenced several poets and composers. Richard Wagner, one of the most famous composers linked with the Rhine, was inspired by the region's tales and scenery. His operas frequently reference Rhine Valley tales and folklore, including as the well-known Rhinegold from his Ring Cycle.

Festivals and Traditions

The Rhine Valley hosts several festivals and cultural events throughout the year. The region celebrates several wine festivals, medieval fairs, and traditional activities that highlight its past. The Rhine in Flames festival, celebrated yearly, is a beautiful event in which castles and towns along the river are lit up with pyrotechnics and torches, creating a wonderful ambiance. Christmas markets in places like as Rüdesheim and Bacharach provide holiday happiness as well as opportunities to learn about local crafts, delicacies, and customs.

What to Expect During Your Visit

Visiting the Rhine Valley is like walking into a novel. The region is a beautiful combination of natural beauty, historical significance, and cultural diversity. Here's what to expect throughout your visit.

Scenic landscapes

The first thing you'll notice is the breathtaking scenery. The Rhine Valley's sceneries vary greatly, from rich vineyards and undulating hills to stunning cliffs and tranquil river vistas. The Rhine Gorge is particularly breathtaking, with its steep hills and several castles that stand above the river. Whether you're visiting the wineries, enjoying a river boat, or hiking the trails, you'll be surrounded by stunning scenery.

Historical Castles and Architecture

The Rhine Valley is home to some of Germany's most recognizable castles and historical structures. Each castle has a distinct history and architectural style. For example, Heidelberg Castle, positioned on a hill overlooking Heidelberg, provides panoramic vistas as well as an insight into the past through its spectacular ruins. Marksburg Castle, one of the best-preserved castles in the region, offers a glimpse into medieval life and architecture.

Wine and Gastronomy

The Rhine Valley is a wine lover's heaven. The region's vineyards produce some of Germany's best wines, and wine tasting is a must-do activity. You may visit local vineyards, take wine excursions, and sample the region's famous Rieslings and other kinds. The wine pairs nicely with the local cuisine, which features traditional dishes that represent the region's culinary heritage. From robust German fare to delicate regional delicacies, the Rhine Valley's culinary culture is guaranteed to please.

Charming towns and villages.

Exploring the cities and villages along the Rhine River is a highlight of any trip. Places like Bacharach, with its medieval beauty and well-preserved architecture, and Rüdesheim, famed for its wine culture and vibrant atmosphere, provide a warm and welcome experience. You may stroll through charming streets, visit small businesses, and experience the kindness of the locals.

Outdoor Activities

If you prefer outdoor activities, the Rhine Valley has a lot to offer. You may go on gorgeous treks along paths with breathtaking river views, or rent a bike and explore the region's cycling routes. River cruises provide a relaxing approach to explore the region, with opportunity to relax and enjoy the views from the water.

Cultural Experiences

Participate in local festivals and activities to get more immersed in the culture. The Rhine Valley's calendar is jam-packed with festivals that honor its traditions and heritage. These events, whether a wine festival, a medieval fair, or a Christmas market, offer a one-of-a-kind opportunity to immerse yourself in the region's vivid culture and dynamic environment.

Practical considerations

When visiting the Rhine Valley, you can anticipate a well-organized and welcoming environment. The region offers a variety of lodgings, ranging from luxurious hotels to lovely guesthouses. Public transportation is widely accessible, making it simple to commute between cities and attractions. Furthermore, English is commonly spoken, particularly in tourist regions, so communication should be rather easy.

To summarize, visitors to the Rhine Valley may expect a rich and varied experience. From its breathtaking scenery and medieval castles to its colorful festivals and wine culture, the area offers an unforgettable and immersive travel experience. Whether you're a history buff, a wine aficionado, or just want to appreciate stunning landscapes and attractive villages, the Rhine Valley has something for everyone.

CHAPTER 2

TOP TOURIST ATTRACTIONS

The Rhine Valley is home to several attractions that highlight its natural beauty, rich history, and cultural heritage. From stunning rock formations to beautiful castles, here's a comprehensive guide to some of the most popular tourist sites in this lovely region.

Lorelei Rock

Overview

Lorelei Rock, also known as Loreley Felsen, is one of the Rhine Valley's most recognizable features. This high slate rock towers 132 meters (433 feet) above the Rhine River in the village of St. Goarshausen. It is located at the narrowest point of the Rhine Gorge, where the river twists abruptly. Lorelei Rock is steeped in tradition and folklore, making it a must-see attraction for tourists.

Legend and Myth

Lorelei Rock is well connected with a mythology of Lorelei, a beautiful siren. Lorelei was said to be a maiden with an exquisite voice who sung from the rock. Her music captivated passing sailors, causing them to get distracted and resulting in disasters. This terrible story has influenced various literary and musical works, adding to the rock's attraction and mystique.

Scenic views

Visitors to Lorelei Rock may enjoy breathtaking views of the Rhine River and the surrounding region. The rock provides a panoramic view of the river running through the verdant countryside, as well as the lovely vineyards and castles dotting the slopes. There are various observation platforms and walking pathways surrounding the rock that allow you to take great photos and completely experience the spectacular environment.

Getting There

The Lorelei Rock is easily accessible from the cities of St. Goarshausen and St. Goar, which are well connected by train and ferry. The region is popular with tourists, and there are well-marked pathways leading to the rock from adjacent cities. If you are going by automobile, parking is accessible, and guided excursions are also available, which provide a fuller understanding of the area's mystique and history.

Heidelberg Castle.

Overview

Heidelberg Castle is one of the most well-known and spectacular castles in Germany. Perched on a hilltop overlooking the city of Heidelberg and the Neckar River, the castle is a stunning example of medieval architecture with a rich historical context. The castle complex is made up of several structures, including the Great Hall, the Old Bridge Gate, and the iconic Heidelberg Tun, a large wine barrel.

Historical significance.

Heidelberg Castle has a long and rich history that dates back to the 13th century. Originally built as a fortification, it was eventually enlarged into a splendid palace for the Electors Palatine. The castle has hosted several historical events and has undergone many modifications throughout the years, including periods of destruction and restoration. Its remains now are a reminder of its previous grandeur and significance.

Architectural Features

The castle's architecture is an intriguing combination of Gothic and Renaissance styles. The Great Hall, with its majestic facade and intricate décor, is the castle complex's main attraction. The Heidelberg Tun, a massive wine barrel capable of holding over 200,000 liters of wine, is another impressive feature. Visitors can visit the castle's different chambers and turrets, each providing insight into the lavish lifestyle of the Electors Palatine.

Visitor Experience

Heidelberg Castle is a renowned tourist site with people from all over the world. The castle may be accessed via a funicular railway or a picturesque hike up the hill. Guided tours are provided, presenting in-depth information on the castle's history and design. The castle grounds also have lovely gardens and panoramic views of the surrounding area, making it an excellent location for unhurried exploring.

Marksburg Castle.

Overview

Marksburg Castle is one of the most well-preserved medieval castles on the Rhine River. It is located near the town of Braubach and sits on a hill overlooking the Rhine, providing a remarkable example of medieval fortification and architecture. Unlike many other castles in the vicinity, Marksburg has never been demolished, and its original features are still mostly intact.

Historical Background.

Marksburg Castle was built in the 13th century and has played an important part in the region's history. It functioned as a stronghold and dwelling for several aristocratic families, and it was strategically located to dominate the Rhine River commerce routes. The castle's location and defenses made it a powerful fortress throughout its existence.

Architectural Features

The castle's building is a great example of medieval defensive design. It has a succession of turrets, battlements, and reinforced walls that give insight into the castle's military history. Inside, visitors may tour the castle's well-preserved halls, such as the great hall, dining rooms, and residential quarters. The castle's interiors are adorned with historical antiques that provide insight into the daily lives of its past residents.

Visiting Marksburg Castle.

Marksburg Castle is a renowned attraction for history buffs and visitors. The castle is accessible via a steep but reasonable trek from the village of Braubach, or by shuttle bus from the town center. Guided tours are provided, presenting in-depth information on the castle's history and design. The castle's lofty position provides breathtaking views of the Rhine River and surrounding landscape.

Rhine Gorge.

Overview

The Rhine Gorge, also known as the Upper Middle Rhine Valley, is a UNESCO World Heritage Site famed for its breathtaking scenery and historical significance. The valley, which stretches around 65 kilometers (40 miles) between the cities of Bingen and Koblenz, is known for its sheer cliffs, rolling vineyards, and several castles.

Scenic Beauty

The Rhine Gorge is known for its magnificent landscape. The river flows through a small valley, surrounded by towering rocks and luscious vineyards. The region's environment is littered with ancient castles and ruins, which add to its beautiful appeal. The Rhine Gorge's spectacular geology and panoramic vistas attract nature enthusiasts and photographers.

Historic and Cultural Sites

The Rhine Gorge is home to a number of significant historical and cultural attractions. In addition to the numerous castles that line the riverbanks, the valley is home to ancient ruins, medieval cities, and picturesque villages. Bacharach and Rüdesheim are well-known for its historical architecture and cultural heritage. Since Roman times, the valley has been a hub of trade and business, and its rich history can be seen in the various landmarks and sites that dot the region.

Activities & Attractions

Visitors to the Rhine Gorge may participate in a range of activities and attractions. River cruises are a popular method to explore the area's natural beauty and historical landmarks, offering a relaxing and stunning perspective of the valley from the river. There are also various hiking and cycling paths that allow you to explore the region's sceneries and admire its breathtaking views. Wine aficionados may visit local vineyards and wineries to sample the region's well-known wines and learn about its viticultural heritage.

Getting Around

The Rhine Gorge is easily accessible by public transit, which includes trains, buses, and ferries. Many visitors choose to explore the area on a river boat, which offers a unique perspective on the region's scenery and attractions. For those who prefer to explore on land, there are various walking and cycling trails that lead to the gorge's magnificent splendor and historical attractions. The region is also accessible by automobile, with plenty of parking in the riverside towns and villages.

the Rhine Valley has a variety of attractions to suit a wide range of interests. Whether you're interested in the stories of Lorelei Rock, the grandeur of Heidelberg Castle, the historical significance of Marksburg Castle, or the natural splendor of the Rhine Gorge, the region offers a memorable experience for every tourist.

Bacharach

Overview

Bacharach is a lovely village on the Rhine River, known for its medieval architecture and attractive surroundings. It is located in the midst of the Rhine Gorge, a UNESCO World Heritage site, and gives visitors a look into the region's rich history and natural beauty. The town's well-preserved ancient structures and stunning vistas make it a popular stop for tourists visiting the Rhine.

Historical significance.

Bacharach's history extends back to Roman times, but it thrived during the Middle Ages as a major commerce city along the Rhine. The town's strategic position made it a vital hub for business and transportation. Many of its structures from this era have survived, giving visitors a feel of the town's medieval charm.

Key Attractions

Bacharach Castle: Perched on a hill above the town, this medieval castle provides panoramic views of the Rhine River and the surrounding valley. It dates back to the 12th century and has undergone partial restoration. The castle grounds are available to tourists, offering an intriguing peek inside medieval fortifications.

St. Peter's Church: This Gothic church, also known as St. Peter's Church, is Bacharach's architectural treasure. Its elaborate brickwork and stunning stained glass windows honor the town's historical and religious traditions.

Bacharach's medieval town walls and gates have survived surprisingly well. Walking along these walls allows you to envision the town's past defenses while also enjoying stunning views of the Rhine.

Historic Half

Timbered buildings: The town is distinguished by its colorful half-timbered buildings that line its small streets. These structures, which date back to the 16th and 17th centuries, add to the town's charming and scenic ambiance.

Activities and Dining

Bacharach is perfect for leisurely walks through its old streets and along the Rhine promenade. There are numerous attractive cafés and restaurants serving local food and Rhine wines. The town also holds a variety of cultural events and festivals throughout the year, such as wine festivals and medieval fairs.

Getting There

Bacharach is easily accessible via train from large towns like as Mainz and Koblenz. The town is also well connected by ferry services on the Rhine River. If you are traveling by automobile, there are parking facilities near the town center.

Koblenz Deutsches Eck.

Overview

Deutsches Eck (German Corner) is a significant landmark in Koblenz, where the Rhine and Moselle rivers meet. This important position is recognized for its impressive monument and panoramic views of the confluence. It is a popular tourist attraction in Koblenz, providing tourists with information on the region's history and culture.

Historic and Cultural Significance

Deutsches Eck is historically noteworthy because it represents the confluence of two main rivers, a key place since ancient times. The area has played an important role in commercial and military history. The monument at Deutsches Eck honors Emperor Wilhelm I and represents German unification.

Key Attractions

The highlight of Deutsches Eck is the towering equestrian statue of Emperor Wilhelm I, which was erected in 1897 and rises 14 meters (46 feet) tall in honor to the first German Emperor of the Second Reich. The statue is mounted on a huge pedestal with intricate reliefs portraying historical themes.

The confluence of the Rhine and Moselle rivers is a breathtaking sight. Visitors may enjoy beautiful views of the rivers' confluence and the surrounding environment. The riverbank promenade is a lovely place to wander and take in the sights.

The Koblenz Cable Car: For a unique view of the confluence, take the Koblenz Cable Car. This journey provides a panoramic view of the rivers, Deutsches Eck, and the surrounding countryside. It connects the town core to the Ehrenbreitstein Fortress on the opposite side of the Rhine.

Activities and Dining

Deutsches Eck is an excellent location for taking a leisurely walk along the river promenade and admiring the sights. The adjacent Altstadt (Old Town) of Koblenz has a wide range of eating alternatives, including typical German restaurants and cafés. The neighborhood also has a number of stores and boutiques.

Getting There

Koblenz is connected by train to large cities like as Cologne and Mainz. Deutsches Eck is a short walk from Koblenz's train station. Local public transportation, including as buses and ferries, provides excellent access to the region.

Rüdesheim am Rhein.

Overview

Rüdesheim am Rhein is a charming village in the Rhine Gorge, famous for its wine production, historic charm, and natural beauty. It is one of the most popular tourist destinations along the Rhine River, with a mix of historical sites, cultural activities, and breathtaking scenery.

Historical significance.

Rüdesheim has a lengthy history going back to Roman times. It became a significant hub for wine production during the Middle Ages, and this legacy continues to this day. The town's historic district is full of well-preserved buildings and small lanes that represent its rich history.

Key Attractions

Drosselgasse, Rüdesheim's famous street, is known for its vibrant atmosphere, traditional wine bars, and ancient half-timbered buildings. It's a terrific place to learn about local culture, drink area wines, and eat traditional German food.

The Niederwald Monument, which stands on a hill overlooking Rüdesheim, honors German unification and the triumph of the German Empire. The monument includes a colossal figure of Germania, which represents the German country. Visitors may get to the monument by a cable car that provides panoramic views of the Rhine Valley.

Rheingau Wine Museum: The Rheingau Wine Museum explores the history and culture of wine production in the region. The exhibitions include winemaking processes, the history of the Rheingau wine area, and the local wine business.

St. Jacob's Church: This ancient church in Rüdesheim's city center is recognized for its stunning Gothic architecture and spectacular interior. It's a calm location to explore that honors the town's historical and religious significance.

Activities and Dining

Rüdesheim is perfect for walking about, with its picturesque streets and historical attractions providing lots to see. The town is well-known for its wine production, and tourists may explore local wineries and vineyards, sample wine, and dine at traditional restaurants. Rüdesheim also holds several festivals and events throughout the year, such as wine festivals and seasonal festivities.

Getting There

Rüdesheim am Rhein may be reached by train from places such as Mainz and Wiesbaden. The town is also accessible via ferry from other Rhine Valley locations. Parking is accessible near the town center for those arriving by vehicle. The Rüdesheim Cable Car provides a picturesque route to the Niederwald Monument, with spectacular views of the Rhine River and surrounding scenery.

Boppard.

Overview

Boppard is a lovely village set along the Rhine River, renowned for its breathtaking scenery and rich history. It is located in the Rhine Gorge, an area known for its natural beauty and historic legacy. The town's lovely streets, antique buildings, and picturesque riverbank setting make it a favorite stop for travelers touring the Rhine Valley.

Historical significance.

Boppard has a history that goes back to Roman times. It was a significant commerce and military center under the Roman Empire because of its strategic location on the Rhine. The town's past is evident in its well-preserved medieval buildings and Roman remains. Boppard's historical significance is further demonstrated by its role as a prominent hub of trade and culture during the Middle Ages.

Key Attractions

Boppard's Old Town is distinguished by its medieval architecture and quaint narrow streets. Highlights include well-preserved half-timbered homes, ancient structures, and small stores. Walking around the Old Town provides insight into the community's rich history and traditional character.

The Four Towers: Boppard has four historic towers that were part of the town's medieval fortifications. These towers, which include the Churfranken Tower and the Römer Tower, provide insight into the town's defensive past as well as spectacular views of the Rhine River and surrounding environment.

St. Severus Church: This Gothic church is a notable landmark in Boppard. Its stunning architecture, which includes a tall spire and elaborate stained glass windows, underlines the town's historical and religious significance.

Rhine Promenade: The Rhine Promenade in Boppard is a lovely promenade along the river with stunning views of the Rhine and neighboring hills. It's an excellent area to unwind, take in the landscape, and breathe fresh air.

Activities and Dining

Boppard is great for viewing historical sights and taking leisurely walks along the Rhine. The town is particularly well-known for its wine production, and tourists may try local wines at a variety of pubs and restaurants. The Rhine Promenade offers a variety of eating alternatives, including classic German restaurants and cafés where you may taste local food while taking in the views of the river.

Getting There

Boppard is easily accessible via train from large towns like as Koblenz and Mainz. The town is also well connected by ferry services on the Rhine River. If you are traveling by automobile, there are parking facilities near the town center.

Burg Eltz.

Overview

Burg Eltz is one of the most well-preserved and scenic castles in Germany, located in the Eltz Forest near the Moselle River. This medieval castle is recognized for its distinctive architecture, historical value, and gorgeous natural surroundings. It remains a popular destination for visitors interested in history, architecture, and scenic beauty.

Historical significance.

Burg Eltz has been in the property of the Eltz family since the 12th century, making it one of the few castles in Germany that has remained in the hands of the same family for almost 800 years. The castle's lengthy history is evident in its well-preserved medieval architecture and the rich collection of antiquities and art inside. The Eltz family played an important part in the region's history, and the castle is a tribute to their power and wealth.

Key Attractions

Burg Eltz is well-known for its fairytale-like look, which includes an ornate facade, turrets, and steeply pitched roofs. The castle is perched on a rocky hill and surrounded by thick woodland, providing a dramatic and magnificent scene. The architecture combines Gothic and Renaissance styles, indicating several eras of building and refurbishment.

The Inner Courtyard: The castle's inner courtyard is a picturesque area surrounded by ancient structures such as the main residence, great hall, and chapel. The courtyard gives a look into medieval castle life and stunning views of the surrounding woodland.

The Treasury: The castle's treasury has a remarkable collection of medieval antiques, such as armor, weapons, and elegant domestic goods. This collection reveals details on the castle's residents' everyday lives and habits.

The Castle Museum: The museum within the castle houses exhibits on the history of Burg Eltz, such as the growth of the castle's architecture, the history of the Eltz family, and many historical items.

Activities and Dining

Visitors to Burg Eltz can take guided tours of the castle's historic chambers and learn about its history. The neighboring woodland provides possibilities for trekking and admiring the natural beauty of the region. There is a small cafe near the castle where tourists may have drinks and light meals while admiring the beautiful surroundings.

Getting There

Burg Eltz is accessible by automobile, with parking provided close to the castle. To approach the castle from the parking lot, tourists must walk via a picturesque woodland route. The ride to Burg Eltz is part of the experience, with stunning views of the forest and the castle itself.

Mainz Cathedral.

Overview

Mainz Cathedral, sometimes called St. Martin's Cathedral, is a historic monument in Mainz, Germany. This stunning church is known for its Romanesque architecture, historical significance, and artistic riches. It is a popular site in Mainz, providing tourists with an insight into the city's rich religious and cultural legacy.

Historical significance.

Mainz Cathedral was built in the tenth century and has had several modifications and extensions throughout the years. It has been a key religious center in the region, hosting important occasions such as the coronation of monarchs. The cathedral's history reflects the city's status as a major hub of Christianity and political power in medieval Europe.

Key Attractions

Mainz Cathedral is a prime example of Romanesque architecture, with enormous stone walls, rounded arches, and elaborate carvings. The cathedral's magnificent exterior and soaring spires make it a visible landmark in the city.

The Cathedral Interior: Inside the cathedral, tourists may view the wonderfully designed nave, which features high vaulted ceilings and intricate columns. The interior has multiple chapels, each with outstanding artworks and sculptures.

The Mainz Cathedral Treasury includes a collection of ecclesiastical items, including as rare reliquaries, vestments, and manuscripts. These pieces shed light on the cathedral's historical and theological importance.

The Romanesque Cloister: The cathedral complex contains a Romanesque cloister, which is a tranquil and lovely place with wonderfully carved columns and arches. The cloister offers a peaceful environment for thought and contemplation.

Activities and Dining

Mainz Cathedral offers guided tours to learn more about its history and architecture. The cathedral is located in the middle of Mainz, with several restaurants and cafés around where tourists may enjoy local food and drinks. Other historic landmarks and activities may be found nearby, making it an excellent starting point for exploring Mainz.

Getting There

Mainz Cathedral is conveniently accessible by train from major towns such Frankfurt and Wiesbaden. It is located in the city center, close to other major attractions and amenities. The cathedral is easily accessible by local public transportation, which includes buses and trams.

CHAPTER 3

OVERVIEW OF ACCOMMODATION OPTIONS.

The Rhine Valley, with its gorgeous scenery and historic charm, has a varied choice of lodging alternatives to suit a variety of tastes and budgets. Whether you want a deluxe getaway, a comfortable, low-cost stay, or a one-of-a-kind boutique experience, the region provides something for everyone. This chapter gives a complete overview of the Rhine Valley's housing possibilities, assisting you in finding the ideal location to stay during your visit.

Luxury Resorts.

For those looking for an extravagant and sumptuous vacation, the Rhine Valley has various luxury resorts that provide first-rate amenities and superb service. These resorts frequently provide breathtaking river views, excellent dining options, and a variety of spa and wellness amenities.

Here are some of the top luxury resorts in the Rhine Valley:

Schloss Reinhartshausen.

Location: Erbach, Hessen.

Overview: Schloss Reinhartshausen is a medieval castle that has been converted into a luxury hotel in the Rhine Valley. This large estate combines historical elegance with contemporary luxury. The castle's magnificent rooms and suites are decorated in medieval style and provide breathtaking views of the neighboring vineyards and the Rhine River.

The resort's amenities include a full-service spa, an indoor pool, and a gourmet restaurant serving local and foreign cuisine. Guests may also enjoy guided wine tours and a variety of outdoor activities such as hiking and cycling.

Highlights: The castle's ancient architecture, paired with its sumptuous interiors, creates an unforgettable stay. The gorgeous environment and high-end amenities make it an excellent choice for guests seeking a premium experience.

Hotel Villa Am Rhein.

Location: Bonn, Nordrhein-Westfalen.

Hotel Villa am Rhein is a beautiful boutique hotel on the Rhine River in Bonn. This magnificent property provides a refined setting, modern amenities, and breathtaking river views. The hotel's elegant decor and customized service provide a pleasant and distinguished atmosphere for guests.

Amenities: The hotel has modern rooms and suites, a fitness center, and a spa with a variety of services. The on-site restaurant serves a range of gourmet cuisine, and the patio offers a gorgeous eating environment with views of the Rhine.

Highlights: Hotel Villa am Rhein's blend of modern conveniences and historic charm, as well as its ideal position on the riverfront, make it an exceptional choice for a delightful stay.

Hotel Kloster Marienhöh.

Location: Langweiler, Rheinland-Pfalz.

Overview: Hotel Kloster Marienhöh, located in a former monastery, provides a tranquil and upmarket refuge in the picturesque Rhine valley. The hotel's unusual location and calm surroundings offer a pleasant respite from the rush and bustle of daily life.

The resort's amenities include a spa and wellness center, an indoor pool, and a fine dining restaurant. Guests can engage in wellness activities such as yoga and meditation, or explore the stunning natural surroundings that surround the resort.

Highlights: With its historical ambiance, modern luxury, and emphasis on wellness, Hotel Kloster Marienhöh is an ideal choice for those seeking relaxation and rejuvenation.

Budget-Friendly Hotels

For guests looking for comfort and convenience without breaking the bank, the Rhine Valley has a variety of budget-friendly hotels. These lodgings provide exceptional value for money, frequently including needed facilities and a handy location.

Here are some top cost-effective options:

Hotel Rheinischer Hof.

Location: Koblenz, Rheinland-Pfalz.

Overview: The Hotel Rheinischer Hof is a popular budget hotel in Koblenz's city center. It provides a pleasant accommodation with convenient access to local attractions and the Rhine River. The hotel's courteous staff and clean, efficient rooms make it a popular choice among budget-conscious guests.

The hotel has free Wi-Fi, continental breakfast, and a bar/lounge area. The rooms are outfitted with modest furniture and provide a pleasant, friendly atmosphere.

Highlights: Hotel Rheinischer Hof's central location and price make it an excellent choice for those wishing to discover Koblenz and the neighboring Rhine Valley without breaking the bank.

Hotel Bergheim.

Location: Bingen am Rhein, Rhineland-Pfalz

Overview: Hotel Bergheim provides affordable lodging in the picturesque town of Bingen am Rhein. The hotel is noted for its nice accommodations, helpful staff, and handy location near the Rhine River.

The hotel has complimentary Wi-Fi, a daily breakfast buffet, and a restaurant that serves traditional German cuisine. The rooms are modest yet comfortable, with all the necessities for a nice stay.

Highlights: Hotel Bergheim's pricing, convenience, and accessibility to local attractions make it a good choice for budget tourists visiting the Rhine Valley.

Hotel Saint-Pierre

Location: Mainz, Rheinland-Pfalz.

Hotel St. Pierre is a budget-friendly hotel in Mainz with easy access to the city's attractions and the Rhine River. The hotel offers modest rooms with an emphasis on price and convenience.

Amenities: The hotel has free Wi-Fi, a complementary breakfast, and plain, clean rooms. Throughout your visit, the pleasant staff is there to assist you with any requirements or recommendations.

Highlights: The hotel's central location and inexpensive costs make it a sensible choice for budget-conscious guests visiting Mainz and touring the Rhein Valley.

Boutique Guesthouses.

Boutique guesthouses provide a more customized and distinctive staying experience than regular hotels. These lodgings frequently have unique décor, local charm, and a more intimate setting.

Here are some of the best boutique guesthouses in the Rhine Valley:

Gästehaus am Rheinufer.

Location: Rüdesheim am Rhein, Rheinland-Pfalz.

Gästehaus am Rheinufer is a delightful boutique hostel on the Rhine River in Rüdesheim. The guesthouse blends modern conveniences with a welcoming, homey environment, making it a popular choice for travelers looking for a customized experience.

Amenities: The guesthouse has free Wi-Fi, a daily breakfast, and spacious rooms with river views. Guests can also enjoy a common living room and a lovely garden.

Highlights: The guesthouse's riverbank position, along with its friendly service and distinct character, make it an unforgettable stay for visitors to Rüdesheim and the Rhine Valley.

Villa Cazal.

Location: Bacharach, Rheinland-Pfalz.

Villa Cazal is a boutique guesthouse located in the beautiful village of Bacharach. This exquisite establishment combines modern comfort and historic charm, with distinctively furnished rooms and a warm environment.

Amenities: The guesthouse offers free Wi-Fi, a gourmet breakfast, and elegantly equipped rooms. Guests can also appreciate the beautiful garden and the guesthouse's closeness to nearby attractions.

Highlights: Villa Cazal's elegant décor, personalized service, and picturesque setting make it an excellent choice for guests looking for a unique and comfortable stay in Bacharach.

Gästehaus Breuer.

Location: Boppard, Rheinland-Pfalz.

Overview: Gästehaus Breuer is a charming boutique hotel in the center of Boppard. The guesthouse provides a welcoming atmosphere, customized service, and comfortable lodgings.

The guesthouse offers free Wi-Fi, a great breakfast, and well-appointed rooms with a cozy atmosphere. The friendly proprietors are delighted to provide local recommendations and guarantee a nice visit.

Highlights: Visitors touring the Rhine Valley will appreciate Gästehaus Breuer's attractive atmosphere, great service, and accessible location in Boppard.

The Rhine Valley has a wide variety of hotel alternatives to suit all preferences and budgets. There is something for everyone, from magnificent resorts with high-end amenities to low-cost hotels and lovely boutique guesthouses. By taking into account your interests and needs, you may choose the ideal spot to stay and maximize your time in this beautiful and historic region.

Unique Stays

The Rhine Valley is well-known for its conventional lodgings as well as its unusual hotel alternatives, which provide a one-of-a-kind and unforgettable experience.

If you're wanting to stay somewhere out of the ordinary, explore these one-of-a-kind lodgings that add an unusual twist to your stay:

Rheinhaus Boat Hotel

Location: Mainz, Rheinland-Pfalz.

Overview: The RheinHaus Boat Hotel provides a one-of-a-kind experience on the Rhine River. Docked in Mainz, this floating hotel blends the ambiance of a regular hotel with the novelty of living on water. The boat's staterooms are well-appointed, with magnificent river views and contemporary facilities.

Amenities: The boat hotel has free Wi-Fi, a restaurant serving local and foreign cuisine, and a sun terrace with a view. The experience includes the gentle swing of the river and the peaceful atmosphere of life on the water.

Highlights: Staying at RheinHaus provides a unique experience with the convenience of modern amenities. The unusual environment and river views make it an unforgettable destination for those looking for something new.

Treehouse in Schloss Eberstein.

Location: Gernsbach, Baden-Württemberg.

Overview: For those who prefer a little adventure, the Treehouse at Schloss Eberstein offers a wonderful and peaceful hideaway amid the treetops. This luxurious treehouse, located on the grounds of a medieval castle, combines nature and refinement in a unique way.

facilities: The treehouse has excellent furniture, a private balcony with woodland views, and all modern facilities such as Wi-Fi and a minibar. Guests also get access to the castle's restaurant and grounds.

Highlights: The mix of a treetop refuge and a medieval castle creates a memorable stay. The serene environment and luxurious accents make for an unforgettable experience in the midst of nature.

Historical Wine Cellar Stays.

Location: Rüdesheim am Rhein, Rheinland-Pfalz.

Overview: Some antique wine cellars in the Rhine Valley have been converted into lovely guesthouses. Staying in one of these cellars allows you to directly experience the region's winemaking legacy, since rooms frequently have original architectural components and wine-themed décor.

facilities: These one-of-a-kind apartments often combine comfortable, rustic comforts with modern facilities. Guests may also enjoy guided tours of the wine cellars and samples of local wine.

Highlights: The historical ambiance and wine-related events provide a thorough exploration of the region's cultural and gastronomic heritage.

Most Recommended Accommodation

Choosing the right place to stay can make your Rhine Valley visit even more enjoyable.

Here are some highly suggested alternatives in several categories that frequently earn great feedback for their quality, service, and unique offerings:

Hotel Schloss Reinhartshausen.

Location: Erbach, Hessen.

Overview: This luxury castle hotel is great for those looking for a royal experience with modern amenities. The castle's beautiful architecture and lovely environs lend a fairytale-like atmosphere.

Why Recommended: Excellent service, high-quality amenities, and the option to stay in a medieval castle make this an excellent choice for luxury travelers.

Hotel Bergheim.

Location: Bingen am Rhein, Rhineland-Pfalz

Overview: Hotel Bergheim is a trustworthy alternative for budget tourists, offering pleasant lodgings and a handy location in a picturesque town.

Why Recommended: It is popular among budget-conscious tourists because to its affordability, inviting atmosphere, and excellent service.

Villa Cazal.

Location: Bacharach, Rheinland-Pfalz.

Overview: This boutique guesthouse is notable for its exquisite décor and individual service. It provides a unique and private stay in one of the Rhine Valley's most lovely villages.

Why Recommended: The combination of design, comfort, and a delightful location in Bacharach make Villa Cazal an excellent choice for people looking for a boutique experience.

Selecting the Right Accommodation for You

The ideal lodging in the Rhine Valley is determined by your particular tastes, budget, and desired experience.

Here's a guide to help you find the best accommodations:

Define your priorities.

Consider what is most essential throughout your visit. Are you seeking for luxury and indulgence, a low-cost choice, or an unforgettable experience? Your priorities will help you restrict your options.

Consider the location.

Consider where you wish to be based. If you want to visit certain towns or sites, book hotels that are centrally placed or have easy access to those places.

Review Amenities

Examine the features offered by various lodgings. For example, if you want a luxurious experience, amenities like a spa, gourmet cuisine, and high-end furniture may be significant. For low-cost accommodations, basic amenities such as free Wi-Fi and breakfast may be adequate.

Read reviews.

Reading visitor reviews can help you understand the level of service, cleanliness, and overall experience. Look for evaluations that emphasize topics relevant to you, such as customer service or specific facilities.

Check for special features.

If you're searching for something special, like a historical location or a stay on a boat, be sure the accommodation fits these requirements. Unique elements might make your journey more unforgettable.

Booking Tips & Tricks.

To guarantee a seamless booking procedure and the greatest value, consider the following tips and methods.

Book in advance.

Booking your hotel in advance, especially during high travel seasons, will help you get the greatest pricing and availability. Popular destinations and luxurious lodgings can rapidly fill up.

Use Comparison Sites.

Use comparison sites to locate the greatest prices and offers. These platforms allow you to compare costs from various booking sites and frequently include customer reviews and ratings.

Look for special offers.

Many hotels and guesthouses provide special specials or packages. Check the accommodation's website or contact them directly to learn about any available bargains, discounts, or packages that might help you enjoy your stay.

Verify cancellation policies.

Before confirming your reservation, examine the cancellation policy. Flexibility is vital in case your trip plans change. Some motels provide free cancellation up to a specific date, which might be beneficial.

Confirm all details.

Please confirm all booking information, including check-in and check-out hours, room type, and any special requests. This helps to prevent any misconceptions upon arriving.

Utilize Loyalty Programs.

If you often stay at specific hotel chains, think about joining their reward programs. These programs frequently provide rewards like accommodation upgrades, discounts, and special offerings.

Following these recommendations and knowing your alternatives will allow you to make an informed selection and locate the accommodation that best meets your needs for a wonderful stay in the Rhine Valley.

CHAPTER 4

ITINERARY FOR DIFFERENT TRAVELERS

The Rhine Valley is a varied location that has something for every sort of tourist. Whether you're planning a simple weekend getaway or an intense cultural experience, this chapter offers specialized itineraries to help you make the most of your trip. Here are four thorough itineraries to accommodate a variety of interests: Weekend Getaway, Cultural Immersion, Outdoor Adventure, and Family-Friendly Trip.

Weekend Getaway.

Day One: Arrival and Exploration

Morning: arrival in Mainz.

Accommodation: Stay at a nice hotel like the Hyatt Regency Mainz or a boutique guesthouse in the city center.

Activity: Start your tour with a leisurely stroll through Mainz's Altstadt (Old Town). Explore the Market Square and observe Mainz Cathedral, which is 1,000 years old.

Afternoon Rhine River Cruise.

Activity: Take a leisurely sail along the Rhine River. Many boat cruises provide stunning views of the valley, including sights like the Lorelei Rock and other castles.

Lunch: Enjoy a small meal on board or in a riverfront café, such as Café Extrablatt.

Evening: Dinner and leisure.

Activity: Return to Mainz and dine at a local restaurant, such as Weinstube Rote Rose, which is famed for its regional cuisine and wine selection.

Accommodation: Spend the night in Mainz.

Day two: Historical and scenic highlights.

Morning at Heidelberg Castle.

Activity: Drive or take the train to Heidelberg (about one hour from Mainz). Explore the iconic Heidelberg Castle, which sits atop a hill and offers breathtaking views of the city and the Neckar River. Don't miss the Great Barrel and the castle's stunning gardens.

Lunch: Visit a local restaurant in Heidelberg's Old Town, such as Schnitzelhaus.

Afternoon, Rüdesheim am Rhein

Activity: Visit Rüdesheim am Rhein (approximately an hour from Heidelberg). Visit the Drosselgasse, a bustling street noted for its wine bars and traditional vibe. Take the cable car to the Niederwald Monument for a panoramic view of the Rhine valley.

Activity: Visit the Rhine Valley Museum or the Wine Museum if time allows.

Evening: Return and relax.

Dinner: Visit a local restaurant in Rüdesheim or return to Mainz for a quiet meal at a different location.

Accommodation: Spend another night in Mainz or Rüdesheim, whichever you want.

Day Three: Departure

Morning, last-minute exploration.

Activity: Have a leisurely breakfast and explore any remaining Mainz attractions, such as the Gutenberg Museum or St. Stephan's Church, which features Chagall windows.

Activity: Take a final stroll along the Rhine River before leaving.

Afternoon: Departure

Activity: Check out of hotel and travel to airport or train station for departure.

Cultural Immersion.

Day 1: Historic and Cultural Insight

Morning, arrival at Koblenz.

Accommodation: Stay at a strategically situated hotel, such as the Mercure Hotel Koblenz.

Activity: Start your exploration at Deutsches Eck, where the Rhine and Moselle rivers converge. Visit the Ehrenbreitstein Fortress across the river, which is accessible via cable car and offers panoramic views.

Afternoon: Koblenz Old Town.

Activity: Explore Koblenz's Old Town. To learn more about the region's history, visit the Basilica of St. Castor and the Romantic Rhine Museum.

Lunch: Visit a classic German restaurant, such as Ratskeller Koblenz.

Evening: Rhine Dinner Cruise.

Activity: Go on a Rhine dinner cruise. Experience local food while admiring the lit vistas of castles and vineyards along the river.

Day 2: Artistic and architectural exploration.

Morning: Mainz and its museums.

Activity: Visit Mainz's Gutenberg Museum to learn about the history of printing. Explore the Mainz State Museum's displays on regional history and art.

Lunch: Have a lunch at a nearby cafe, such as Breidenbacher Hof.

Afternoon in Wiesbaden

Activity: Travel to Wiesbaden (approximately 30 minutes from Mainz) to visit the Kurhaus, a beautiful spa facility, and the neighboring Casino. Explore the Museum Wiesbaden's collection of art and natural history displays.

Activity: Walk down the lovely Wilhelmstraße and see the architecture of the old buildings.

Evening: Cultural Evening in Wiesbaden.

Dinner: Visit a Wiesbaden restaurant that serves both local and foreign food, such as Restaurant Ente.

Activity: Depending on your preferences, you may attend a play at the Wiesbaden Theatre or spend a relaxing evening in one of the city's attractive parks.

Day 3: Exploring the vineyards

Morning, Rheingau Wine Region

Activity: Travel to the Rheingau wine area (approximately an hour from Wiesbaden). Visit a classic winery, such as Schloss Vollrads or Kloster Eberbach, for a tour and tasting.

Lunch: Eat at a local wine tavern, such as Weinhaus Bluhm.

Afternoon, Rüdesheim am Rhein

Activity: Spend the afternoon in Rüdesheim am Rhein, visiting the Wine Museum or having a leisurely stroll down Drosselgasse.

Activity: Visit Siegfried's Mechanical Music Cabinet, a museum specializing on mechanical musical instruments.

Evening: Return and relax.

Dinner: Return to Koblenz or Mainz and dine at your preferred restaurant.

Accommodation: Stay the night in Koblenz or Mainz.

Day Four: Departure

Morning: Final exploration.

Activity: Have breakfast and enjoy a final tour around the city. Visit any last-minute cultural attractions or stores.

Afternoon departure: Check out and head to the airport or train station.

Outdoor Adventure.

Day 1: Arrival, Scenic Hikes

Morning: arrival in Boppard.

Accommodation: Stay at a local guesthouse or hotel, such as the Hotel Bergschlösschen.

Activity: Begin your journey with a trek on the Boppard Loop Trail. This 13-kilometer circular walk provides breathtaking views of the Rhine River and its neighboring vineyards.

Afternoon Outdoor Activities

Activity: Rent a bike and enjoy the Rhine Valley's picturesque riding routes. The journey from Boppard to Koblenz is scenic and rich in history.

Lunch: Take a picnic along the river or eat at a riverside café.

Evening: Relaxation.

Dinner: Have a full supper at a local restaurant, such as Restaurant Sesselbahn.

Accommodation: Stay the night in Boppard.

Day 2: Explore the Rhine Gorge

Morning: hike the Rhine Gorge.

Activity: Visit the Rhine Gorge, a UNESCO World Heritage site noted for its spectacular scenery. Hike a portion of the Rheinsteig Trail, which runs beside the Rhine and provides spectacular views of the river, castles, and vineyards.

Lunch: Stop at a local restaurant or café in one of the picturesque towns along the road.

Afternoon activity: Take a boat cruise on the Rhine River to see the breathtaking sights from a fresh perspective. Many trips include views of prominent sights including Lorelei Rock and numerous castles.

Activity: For a more active river experience, consider kayaking or canoeing.

Evening: Local cuisine.

Dinner: Visit a local restaurant renowned for its regional food, such as the Rheinhotel Vier Jahreszeiten in Boppard.

Accommodation: Return to your lodging for a relaxing night.

Day three: Adventure in the Forest

Morning: Hike in the Taurus Mountains

Activity: Visit the Taunus Mountains, located near Wiesbaden. Explore the region's various hiking paths, such as the Feldberg or Großer Feldberg, which provide stunning vistas and opportunities to see native flora and wildlife.

Lunch: Have a lunch at a mountain resort or bring a picnic.

Afternoon: Adventure Park.

Activity: For an adrenaline-pumping experience, head to a local adventure park like Taunus Wunderland, which offers outdoor sports like zip-lining and climbing courses.

Activity: For a more peaceful afternoon, visit one of the nearby villages or take a nice walk through the forest.

Evening: Return and relax.

Dinner: Return to your base and dine at a nearby restaurant.

Accommodation: Stay overnight in Boppard or another nearby town.

Day Four: Departure

Morning: Final exploration.

Activity: Have a leisurely breakfast before taking a last stroll or bike ride along the Rhine River.

Afternoon: Departure

Activity: Check out of your accommodations and go to your departure location.

Family-Friendly Travel

Day One: Arrival and Family Fun.

Morning, arrival at Koblenz.

Accommodation: Stay at a family-friendly hotel, such as Park Inn by Radisson Koblenz.

Activity: Begin your journey by visiting the Deutsches Eck, where youngsters may enjoy the wide areas and observe the boats on the river.

Afternoon at Ehrenbreitstein Fortress

Activity: Take the cable car to the Ehrenbreitstein Fortress. Explore the interactive exhibitions and see the panoramic vistas. The fortress frequently holds family-oriented events and activities.

Lunch: Eat in the castle café or a local restaurant.

Evening: relaxing. Dinner

Dinner: Have a family supper at a nearby restaurant, such as the Steigenberger Hotel Restaurant.

Accommodation: Stay the night in Koblenz.

Day 2: Fun and Learning.

Morning: Rhine and Moselle rivers.

Activity: Take a family-friendly river tour that includes entertainment and educational discussion about the area's history.

Lunch: Eat on the ship or in a riverfront café.

Afternoon: Visit local attractions.

Activity: Visit a family destination, such as the Zoo Neuwied, which is only a short drive from Koblenz. The zoo has a variety of animals and recreational spaces for children.

Activity: Alternatively, visit the Rhein-Mosel-Halle, which frequently hosts family-friendly activities and exhibitions.

Evening: leisure time.

Dinner: Head to a family-friendly restaurant with a broad cuisine, such as Family Restaurant Koblenz.

Accommodation: Return to your hotel for a relaxing night's sleep.

Day 3: Exploring the outdoors

Morning: Outdoor Adventure.

Activity: Visit the Rheingau area for outdoor pleasure. Visit local parks and hiking routes that are appropriate for children.

Lunch: Have a picnic or eat at a nearby restaurant.

Afternoon: Theme Park Fun.

Activity: Spend the afternoon at a neighboring theme park, such as Phantasialand or Europa-Park. These parks provide a variety of attractions that are appropriate for all ages.

Activity: If theme parks are not an option, consider visiting a nearby adventure playground or educational farm.

Evening: Family dinner.

Dinner: Eat at a family-friendly restaurant in the region.

Accommodation: Return to your lodging for the night.

Day Four: Departure

Morning: Final Family Activity.

Activity: Have a leisurely breakfast before visiting a last family-friendly destination, such as a neighborhood playground or a nearby park.

Afternoon: Departure

Activity: Check out of your hotel and proceed to your departure destination.

These itineraries provide a varied selection of activities, guaranteeing that every tourist will find something interesting in the Rhine Valley. Whether you want a quick escape, cultural immersion, outdoor adventure, or a family-friendly vacation, the Rhine Valley has something for everyone.

Budget Travel

Budget travel does not mean missing out on the Rhine Valley's charm and excitement. With careful planning and a few money-saving measures, you may have a memorable time without breaking the bank.

Day 1: Affordable Arrival and Exploration

Morning, arrival at Koblenz.

Accommodation: Stay at a low-cost hotel or hostel, such as the A&O Koblenz, or at a budget guesthouse.

Activity: Begin with a self-guided walking tour of Koblenz. Explore the Deutsches Eck, where the Rhine and Moselle rivers converge. The neighborhood is free to explore and has plenty of historic charm.

Afternoon: Scenic and Free Activities.

Activity: Visit Ehrenbreitstein Fortress. While an access charge may be required, the surrounding surroundings and views from the stronghold are free to enjoy.

Lunch: Get a cheap meal at a nearby café or bakery. Koblenzer Brauerei, for example, serves reasonably priced meals and beverages.

Evening: Budget dining

Dinner: Visit a local restaurant with affordable selections or get take-out from a local store.

Accommodation: Spend the night in a low-cost lodging facility.

Day 2: Exploring the Rhine on a Budget

Morning: Free and Low-cost Sightseeing

Activity: Visit Boppard, which is noted for its free walking routes along the Rhine. The Boppard Loop Trail provides spectacular vistas at no cost.

Lunch: Bring a picnic or buy a cheap lunch from a nearby grocery.

Afternoon: Cost-effective Activities.

Activity: Take the train or bus to explore the Rhine Valley's lovely towns. Public transit is typically less expensive than hiring a car. Visit places like Rüdesheim and Bacharach, where you may roam about and enjoy the old streets for free.

Activity: If a low-cost boat cruise is available, join it. Some local firms provide shorter, less costly river tours.

Evening: Local and inexpensive dining

Dinner: Have a dinner at a local cafe or beer garden at a reasonable price.

Accommodation: Return to your cheap hotel in Koblenz or another town.

Day 3: Affordable Adventures

Morning: Explore Mainz.

Activity: Travel to Mainz by rail or bus and then tour the city on foot. Visit the Gutenberg Museum (check for special discount days) or the Mainz Cathedral. The cathedral is free to enter and provides insight into local history.

meal: Choose a low-cost meal from a neighborhood café or street food seller.

Afternoon Budget-Friendly Activities

Activity: Visit the Mainz State Museum or take a stroll around the Altstadt (Old Town), all of which provide free or low-cost activities.

Activity: Walk along the Rhine River or visit a nearby park.

Evening: Affordable. Farewell

Dinner: Have a last dinner at a low-cost restaurant or buy ingredients for a home-cooked meal.

Accommodation: Spend the final night at your cheap hotel.

Day Four: Departure

Morning: Last Minute Savings

Activity: Have a leisurely breakfast and enjoy a last stroll through the city, possibly stopping at a local market for affordable gifts.

Afternoon: Departure

Activity: Check out and proceed to your departure location.

Solo Traveler's Guide.

Traveling alone in the Rhine Valley may be a fulfilling and enriching experience. From self-discovery to meeting new people, here's how to get the most out of your solo vacation.

Day One: Solo Exploration and Socialization

Morning: Arrival and orientation.

Accommodation: Stay in a lone traveler-friendly hotel or guesthouse, such as the A&O Koblenz, or a boutique guesthouse with communal facilities for socializing.

Activity: Start your solo adventure with a walking tour of Koblenz. Visit the Deutsches Eck and explore the region at your leisure.

Afternoon: Join a Group Activity.

Activity: Participate in a group trip or a river cruise. Many firms provide small group trips, which are perfect for single travelers looking to meet people.

Lunch: Have a meal at a café where you can interact with locals and other travelers.

Evening: Social dining.

Dinner: Visit a communal or popular restaurant, such as Café Extrablatt, where solitary travelers are generally accepted.

Accommodation: Spend the evening at your hostel or guesthouse. Participate in any social activities or meetings hosted by the hostel.

Day 2: Cultural immersion.

Morning: Explore Rüdesheim.

Activity: Make a day excursion to Rüdesheim. Explore Drosselgasse and see the Niederwald Monument. The cable car trip provides an opportunity to meet other people.

Lunch: Eat at a local restaurant or join a group for a wine tasting.

Afternoon: Cultural Experience

Activity: Visit a nearby museum or historical place, such as the Wine Museum or Siegfried's Mechanical Music Cabinet.

Activity: Rent a bike and explore the Rhine Valley at your own leisure.

Evening: Solo and social.

supper: Have supper at a neighborhood restaurant recognized for its friendly atmosphere.

Activity: Visit local bars and cafés, where you may meet other visitors or residents.

Day three: scenic and relaxing.

Morning: Hike or bike through Boppard.

Activity: Spend the morning hiking or biking on the Boppard Loop Trail. It's an excellent approach to appreciate nature while also reflecting.

Lunch: Bring a picnic or dine at a nearby cafe.

Afternoon: Relax and reflect.

Activity: Go on a leisurely Rhine cruise or rest at a nearby spa.

Activity: Browse local markets and stores for unusual treasures and gifts.

Evening: Reflective. Dinner

Dinner: Head to a restaurant with a view, such as the Rheinhotel Vier Jahreszeiten.

Accommodation: Return to your lodgings for a relaxing evening.

Day Four: Departure

Morning: Final exploration.

Activity: Enjoy a leisurely breakfast before taking a last walk around Koblenz or Mainz to reflect on your solo adventure.

Afternoon: Departure

Activity: Check out and get to the departure place.

Romantic getaways.

The Rhine Valley is a great romantic getaway, with breathtaking scenery, quaint villages, and personal encounters. Here's how to plan a wonderful romantic holiday.

Day One: Romantic Arrival and Dinner.

Morning: Arrival at Bacharach

Accommodation: Stay at a romantic hotel or guesthouse, such as the Hotel Burg Stahleck, which has beautiful views and a kind ambiance.

Activity: Walk through the scenic streets of Bacharach, which is famous for its well-preserved medieval architecture.

Afternoon Scenic Cruise.

Activity: Enjoy a romantic river trip on the Rhine. Many cruises have food choices as well as stunning views of the valley.

Lunch: Have a small meal on the ship or at a riverfront café.

Evening: romantic dinner.

supper: Enjoy a candlelight supper at a nearby restaurant with a view, such as Restaurant Zur Krone in Bacharach.

Accommodation: Return to your wonderful hotel for a comfortable night.

Day two: Scenic beauty and relaxation.

Morning: Explore Rüdesheim.

Activity: Visit Rüdesheim and discover the lovely Drosselgasse. Visit the Niederwald Monument and ride the cable car for a panoramic view of the Rhine Valley.

Lunch: Have a romantic lunch at a classic wine tavern, like Weinhaus Bluhm.

Afternoon: Wine tasting and relaxation.

Activity: Go to a nearby winery for a private wine tasting. The Rheingau region boasts stunning vineyards and intimate tastings.

Activity: Relax in a spa or wellness facility, if one is available.

Evening: An intimate dinner

Dinner: Dine at a great restaurant, such as the Schloss Reinhartshausen in Eltville, which is noted for its magnificent environment and outstanding cuisine.

Accommodation: Stay at a charming hotel or guesthouse in the region.

Day Three: Historical Romance

Morning at Heidelberg Castle.

Activity: Go to Heidelberg and tour the Heidelberg Castle. The castle boasts breathtaking vistas and a rich history, making it ideal for a romantic adventure.

Lunch: Have lunch at a lovely café in Heidelberg's Old Town.

Afternoon: Romantic stroll

Activity: Take a romantic stroll down the Philosophenweg (Philosopher's Walk), which offers beautiful views of Heidelberg and the Neckar River.

Activity: Visit local stores or take a relaxing coffee break at one of Heidelberg's beautiful cafés.

Evening: Cozy Dinner

Dinner: Eat in a quiet, intimate restaurant in Heidelberg, such as Zum Güld.

enen Schaf.

lodging: Relax in your romantic lodging for the evening.

Day Four: Departure

Early Morning: Final Romantic Moments.

Activity: Have a leisurely breakfast before taking a last stroll around the gorgeous streets or a nearby park.

Afternoon: Departure

Activity: Check out and proceed to your departure location.

These itineraries cater to a variety of travel styles, ensuring that you can experience the finest of the Rhine Valley whether you're on a budget, traveling solo, or on a romantic getaway. With a little forethought, you can make the most of your vacation and create lasting memories.

CHAPTER 5

HOW TO GET THERE

The Rhine Valley, a gorgeous region straddling Germany, France, and Switzerland, provides a variety of transportation alternatives for tourists. Whether you choose to fly, take the train, drive, or arrive by boat, this chapter gives a detailed reference on traveling to the Rhine Valley and exploring the area.

By Air.

The Rhine Valley is easily accessible by flight, thanks to the region's multiple international airports. The most popular airports for travelers visiting the Rhine Valley are in large towns like as Frankfurt, Cologne, and Strasbourg.

Frankfurt Airport (FRA) is located near Frankfurt, Germany, approximately 120 kilometers / 75 miles from the Rhine Valley. It is one of Europe's busiest airports, with numerous international and domestic flights. It offers a variety of amenities and services, including vehicle rentals and direct train access to the Rhine Valley.

Rhine Valley transportation: A direct train from Frankfurt Airport connects to various Rhine Valley sites. The travel to Koblenz or Mainz usually takes about 1 to 1.5 hours. Alternatively, you may hire a car at the airport and enjoy a picturesque drive along the Rhine.

Cologne Bonn Airport (CGN) is located near Cologne, Germany, approximately 60 kilometers (37 miles) from the Rhine Valley.

Description: Cologne Bonn Airport offers both domestic and international flights. It is closer to the northern portion of the Rhine Valley, making it an excellent alternative for those visiting places like as Bonn and Koblenz.

Transportation to the Rhine Valley: You may get there by rail or vehicle. The rail travel to places like Bonn or Koblenz takes around 30 minutes to an hour. Car rentals are available at the airport, providing a more flexible travel alternative.

Strasbourg Airport (SXB) is located near Strasbourg, France, approximately 100 kilometers (62 miles) from the Rhine Valley. It mostly serves European destinations. It's an excellent starting place for travelers interested in the French side of the Rhine Valley.

Transportation to the Rhine Valley: From Strasbourg, you may take a train to Mainz or Koblenz, which takes 1.5 to 2 hours. Rental cars are also available at the airport.

Basel-Mulhouse Airport (BSL/MLH) is located near Basel, Switzerland, approximately 150 kilometers (93 miles) from the Rhine Valley.

Description: Basel-Mulhouse Airport services the borders of Switzerland, France, and Germany. It provides a variety of foreign flights.

Getting to the Rhine Valley: From Basel, you may take a train to Koblenz or Mainz, which takes around 2-3 hours. Rental cars are available for a more direct trip.

Tips for Air Travel:

Book flights in advance to get the best deals. Consider flying to less congested airports for potentially cheaper rates.

Connections: To make your travel to the Rhine Valley more efficient, look into rail or vehicle rental alternatives at your arrival airport.

By Train.

Traveling by rail is a popular and convenient method to see the Rhine Valley. The region is well-connected by a large train network, with several picturesque lines providing comfortable and convenient transportation alternatives.

ICE trains connect major German cities, such as Frankfurt, Cologne, and Düsseldorf, with the Rhine Valley. These trains provide high-speed travel and comfort, making them a good alternative for getting to the Rhine Valley swiftly.

Thalys and Eurostar: Thalys and Eurostar trains connect international passengers from Paris and Brussels to the Rhine Valley, frequently stopping in important German towns along the way.

Regional Express (RE) trains connect small villages and cities in the Rhine Valley. They provide regular service and are perfect for accessing places such as Koblenz, Rüdesheim, and Bacharach.

S-Bahn (S-Bahn Rhein-Ruhr and S-Bahn Rhein-Main): These suburban trains connect the Rhine Valley and adjacent areas, making it convenient to commute between cities and towns.

Major Train Stations in the Rhine Valley:

Koblenz Hauptbahnhof (HB)) is a primary hub that connects large cities and smaller locations.

Mainz Hauptbahnhof (HB): Connects to other German cities as well as numerous Rhine Valley locations.

Heidelberg Hauptbahnhof (HB) serves the Heidelberg region and provides access to the Rhine Valley.

Tips for Train Travel:

Buy tickets in advance to get the best deals. Consider utilizing regional day passes or train cards to save money.

Scenic roads: For stunning views of the valley, choose scenic roads along the Rhine River, such as the route between Koblenz and Bingen.

Reservations: While regional trains seldom require reservations, high-speed trains and long-distance routes frequently benefit from seat reservations.

By Car.

Driving to the Rhine Valley provides freedom and allows you to explore the region at your own speed. The area is accessible via main roads and has picturesque excursions along the Rhine River.

Driving directions:

From Frankfurt, use the A61 highway towards Koblenz or the A5 towards Heidelberg. Both roads provide easy access to significant Rhine Valley sites.

From Cologne, take the A61 south to destinations such as Bonn and Koblenz. The route provides stunning views of the Rhine River and the surrounding landscape.

From Strasbourg, take the A35 highway to the German border, then connect to the A5 motorway towards Heidelberg or the A61 towards Koblenz.

To get to the Rhine Valley, use the A35 and A5 highways north from Basel. The journey passes through stunning scenery and attractive villages.

To drive safely, it's important to be aware of local traffic rules and regulations. In Germany, speed restrictions are carefully enforced, and parking in city areas may be limited.

Toll Roads: Some roadways may charge tolls. Toll payments must be made in cash or with a credit card.

Navigation: Use a GPS or navigation app to navigate your way around and discover gorgeous pathways along the Rhine River.

Parking in city centers may be problematic, particularly in Koblenz and Mainz. Look for authorized parking places or take public transit throughout the city.

Scenic Areas: Several towns and attractions provide parking for visitors. Check local listings for parking choices near major locations.

By Boat.

Arriving by boat offers a unique and scenic approach to the Rhine Valley, with views of the region's picturesque landscapes and historic landmarks.

River Cruises:

Rhine River Cruises: Several firms provide river cruises along the Rhine, giving a relaxing and scenic opportunity to explore the valley. The length of a cruise might range from a single day to many days.

Popular Cruise Lines: Viking River Cruises, Avalon Waterways, and AmaWaterways are some of the most well-known river cruise lines that operate on the Rhine. These cruises provide elegance and comfort, with numerous itineraries that visit significant Rhine Valley locations.

Day cruises on the Rhine River allow for exploration of specific portions and visits to cities like Bacharach and Rüdesheim.

Sightseeing Cruises: Many Rhine cities, like Koblenz and Boppard, provide sightseeing cruises that highlight the river's beautiful splendor and historical sites.

Port Locations:

Koblenz: The primary river port is near the Deutsches Eck, providing convenient access to the city center and other attractions.

Boppard: Boppard's port is centrally positioned, making it easy to explore the town and its beautiful environs.

Rüdesheim: Rüdesheim's port is adjacent to the town center, giving visitors easy access to sights like as the Drosselgasse and the Niederwald Monument.

Tips for Boat Travel:

Book river cruises and tours in advance, especially during high seasons. Many firms provide online booking alternatives.

Weather: Prepare for a variety of weather situations. Bring proper attire, including a light jacket or raincoat.

Sightseeing: Relax and enjoy the scenery by taking a boat excursion. Many trips include commentary or guides to improve your experience.

Traveling to the Rhine Valley is a pleasant experience with a variety of transportation alternatives. Whether you choose to fly, take the train, drive, or arrive by boat, each route has certain advantages that can improve your entire travel experience. With careful planning and consideration of your tastes, you may have a smooth trip to one of Europe's most picturesque and culturally rich places.

CHAPTER 6

THE BEST TIME TO VISIT.

The ideal time to visit the Rhine Valley depends on a variety of factors, including weather, seasonal events, and personal tastes. The region's attractiveness may be enjoyed all year, but recognizing seasonal fluctuations and unique events will help you make the most of your visit.

Seasonal Overview.

The Rhine Valley has a moderate environment with various seasons that each provide a distinctive experience.

Here's an overview of what you may anticipate throughout the year:

Spring (March – May)

Weather: Springtime brings gentler temperatures and blossoming flowers. Daytime temperatures normally vary between 10°C and 20°C (50°F to 68°F). It's an excellent time to watch the valley come alive with brilliant hues.

Benefits: Spring is good for outdoor activities such as hiking and sightseeing, with less people than summer. The weather is pleasant, and you may see the beautiful surroundings as flowers and trees blossom.

Events: Spring brings a variety of local events and marketplaces, including the Mainz Spring Fair and the Rüdesheim Wine Festival.

Summer (June-August)

Weather: The Rhine Valley experiences mild summers, with temperatures ranging from 20°C to 30°C (68°F to 86°F). This is the main tourist season, with long, bright days and relaxing evenings.

Benefits: Summer provides ideal weather for outdoor sports, river cruises, and touring historic places. Festivals and events are in full swing, and many sites offer longer hours.

Events: The Rhine in Flames event, which features amazing fireworks displays, is a highlight of the summer season. Other prominent events include the Bacharach Wine Festival and a number of local music and cultural festivals.

Autumn (September–November)

Weather: Autumn provides colder temps and vibrant greenery. Daytime temperatures range between 10°C and 20°C (50°F to 68°F). The weather may be erratic, with intermittent rain and fog.

Benefits: Autumn is a more tranquil season to come, with less visitors and stunning fall colors. The grape harvest and wine festivals take place during this season, making it an ideal time for wine tasting.

Events: The Wine Harvest Festivals, held in Rüdesheim and Bacharach, are notable highlights. This season also features typical Oktoberfest events in a variety of places.

Winter (December - February).

Weather: The Rhine Valley has frigid winters, with temperatures ranging from -1°C to 8°C (30°F to 46°F). Snowfall is possible, but not guaranteed. During this time, the environment is calm and lovely.

Benefits: Winter provides a more calm atmosphere with less tourists. It's the perfect time to cuddle up in a warm guesthouse or visit sparkling Christmas markets.

Events: Christmas markets in locations such as Koblenz and Mainz are popular, offering local crafts, festive snacks, and holiday happiness. Winter also provides the opportunity to enjoy the Rhine Valley's beautiful grandeur in a more tranquil atmosphere.

Tips for Seasonal Travel:

Pack suitable attire for the season. Layering is good in the spring and fall, whereas summer demands lighter clothes and winter requires heated layers.

Accommodation: Make reservations in advance, particularly during high seasons such as summer and Christmas. Off-peak seasons might provide reduced pricing and increased availability.

Festivals & Events

The Rhine Valley is noted for its dynamic cultural scene, which includes a number of festivals and events hosted throughout the year. These festivals highlight local customs, arts, and cuisine, providing a special depth to your stay.

Spring festivals include the Mainz Spring Fair (April), which offers rides, games, and food vendors. It heralds the start of the festival season and has a family-friendly environment.

Rüdesheim Wine Festival (May): A celebration of local wines in the picturesque village of Rüdesheim. The event features wine tastings, live music, and food vendors, bringing wine aficionados from all across the region.

Summer Festivals:

Rhine in Flames (May-September): A stunning festival along the Rhine River, with fireworks displays and lit ships. The event takes place in numerous places, including Koblenz and Boppard.

Bacharach Wine event (August): This event, held in the medieval town of Bacharach, celebrates the region's winemaking legacy with tastings, live entertainment, and traditional cuisine.

Cologne Summer Carnival (July): While not located in the Rhine Valley, this carnival in adjacent Cologne is a huge festival that includes parades, music, and street parties. It's a lively complement to any summer excursion.

Autumn celebrations:

Wine Harvest Festivals (September-October): Rhine Valley villages like Rüdesheim and Bacharach have grape harvest celebrations with wine tastings, traditional music, and local food.

Oktoberfest (September-October): Celebrated in numerous places, Oktoberfest provides a taste of Bavarian culture through beer, traditional music, and festive costumes.

Winter Festivals:

Christmas Markets (December): The Rhine Valley's Christmas markets are popular for their joyful ambiance. Highlights include the Koblenz Christmas Market, the Mainz Christmas Market, and the Rüdesheim Christmas Market, which all provide crafts, food, and seasonal pleasure.

New Year's Eve Celebrations: Many municipalities organize New Year's Eve festivities, such as fireworks displays and parties. The mood is celebratory, and it's an excellent way to begin the new year.

Tips for Festival Visits:

Plan ahead of time by checking festival dates and booking lodgings, since popular events might attract enormous crowds.

Local Customs: To make the most of your festival experience, learn about the local customs and traditions.

Weather Considerations.

Understanding the weather is critical for planning your Rhine Valley trip since it affects activities, clothes, and overall experience. The climate in the region varies greatly depending on the season.

Spring weather often brings pleasant temperatures ranging from 10°C to 20°C (50°F to 68°F). Early spring may be colder, with temperatures gradually rising.

Precipitation: Spring can be rainy, so pack an umbrella and weatherproof gear.

Outdoor Activities: The countryside is flowering and the attractions are less crowded, making it ideal for trekking and exploration.

Summer temperatures typically range from 20°C to 30°C (68°F to 86°F), with rare heatwaves raising temperatures even higher.

Precipitation: Summer is mostly dry, however small rain showers may occur. Light rain gear could be beneficial.

Outdoor Activities: Ideal for river cruising, touring, and visiting festivals. Pack sunscreen, sunglasses, and lightweight clothes.

Autumn weather:

Temperatures vary from 10°C to 20°C (50°F to 68°F), progressively dropping throughout the season.

Precipitation: The weather can be unpredictable, with an increased risk of rain and mist. Pack layers and a wet jacket.

Outdoor Activities: Perfect for enjoying the fall colors and attending wine harvest festivals. Prepare for chilly evenings.

Winter temperatures range between -1°C and 8°C (30°F to 46°F). Snowfall is possible, but not guaranteed.

Precipitation: Expect chilly weather with some snow and rain. Warm clothes, especially a heavy coat, gloves, and a cap, are required.

Outdoor Activities: Visit Christmas markets and admire winter scenery. Be prepared for icy weather and few daylight hours.

To remain up-to-date on current weather conditions, use apps or check predictions before traveling.

Layering: Dress in layers to adjust to changing weather, especially in the spring and fall.

Weather Related Events: Certain outdoor events or activities may be weather dependent. Prepare backup plans in the event of a disaster.

The ideal time to visit the Rhine Valley is determined by your preferred weather, events, and activities. Each season provides its own distinct experience, from bustling summer festivities to tranquil winter vistas. Understanding seasonal differences and preparing properly can help you have a memorable and pleasurable stay to this wonderful location.

CHAPTER 7

DURATION OF STAY.

The length of your stay in the Rhine Valley has a big impact on how much you appreciate and explore the region. Whether you're planning a quick visit or a longer investigation, knowing how to maximize your time can help you make the most of your vacation. This chapter makes recommendations for the best length of stay and recommends itineraries for various lengths.

Recommended length of stay

Short Visits (2-3 days)

Even if you only have a limited amount of time, you may still see some of the Rhine Valley's main attractions. A two- to three-day stay is great if you're passing through the area or have a limited time. Here's what you can cover in this little window.

Day 1: Concentrate on one town or city to obtain a sense of local culture. Koblenz or Rüdesheim am Rhein are excellent choices. Explore the town's historical landmarks, take a picturesque river boat, and eat at a local restaurant.

Day 2: Explore surrounding sights or towns. In Koblenz, you may visit Deutsches Eck and Ehrenbreitstein Fortress. Consider going wine tasting in Rüdesheim and seeing Siegfried's Mechanical Musical Instrument Museum.

Day 3: Use your final day for a picturesque drive or a quick trip to another town. If you're in Koblenz, consider visiting Boppard. While in Rüdesheim, a simple trip to Bacharach might give extra historical and picturesque pleasures.

Moderate stay (4-6 days).

A stay of four to six days provides for a more unhurried tour of the Rhine Valley. This period allows you to see a wider number of sights and towns, delivering a more complete experience.

Days 1-2: Begin with a big city, such as Koblenz. Explore Deutsches Eck, Ehrenbreitstein Fortress, and Old Town. Take a river cruise and consider a day excursion to the Rhine Gorge.

Days 3-4: Continue to Rüdesheim am Rhein, where you may see ancient buildings and learn about wine culture. Visit the Drosselgasse for its bustling atmosphere and to sample local wines. Consider visiting the Niederwald Monument for panoramic views.

Days 5-6: Spend the days touring local towns like Bacharach and Boppard. Explore Bacharach's historic streets and explore Marksburg Castle. In Boppard, take a lovely cable car ride and wander along the river.

Extended Stay (7+ days)

A week-long visit provides for a thorough exploration of the Rhine Valley, with plenty of time to experience a variety of historical, cultural, and natural sites.

Days 1-2: Begin your vacation in Koblenz, taking in important sights such as Deutsches Eck, Ehrenbreitstein Fortress, and the Old Town. Enjoy a relaxing river trip.

Days 3–4: Travel to Rüdesheim am Rhein. Spend time experiencing the wine culture, historic landmarks, and picturesque vistas. Take the cable car to the Niederwald Monument.

Days 5–6: Visit adjacent towns like Bacharach and Boppard. Take time to explore the castles, charming streets, and river vistas. Include visits to lesser sights and local restaurants.

Days 7 and up: Spend any leftover days exploring additional sights like Burg Eltz and Mainz Cathedral. If you enjoy seeing historical sights, consider taking a day trip to Heidelberg. You might also go on leisurely river cruises or hikes in the neighboring locations.

Tips for Determining Duration:

Consider your interests and priorities to determine the appropriate length of stay. History aficionados may want to spend more time visiting castles and museums, whilst wine enthusiasts may choose to explore vineyards and local festivals.

Travel Pace: Consider how quickly you prefer to move between places. If you prefer a leisurely pace with plenty of time to explore each attraction, book a longer stay.

Recommended Itineraries for Various Lengths

To make the most of your time in the Rhine Valley, here are some suggested itineraries for varying durations of stay. These itineraries aim to strike a balance between sightseeing, leisure, and discovery.

2-Day Itinerary

Day 1 in Koblenz

Morning: Arrive in Koblenz and settle into your accommodations. Begin your day with a visit to Deutsches Eck, where the Rhine and Moselle rivers meet. Explore the Ehrenbreitstein Fortress across the river to get panoramic views of the city.

Afternoon: Explore Koblenz's Old Town, including the Church of Our Lady and Schlosspark. Enjoy lunch at a nearby café.

In the evening, take a leisurely Rhine River boat to enjoy the gorgeous scenery and ancient structures. Have supper at a neighborhood restaurant and enjoy the evening atmosphere.

Day Two: Rüdesheim am Rhein.

Morning: Travel to Rüdesheim am Rhein by car or rail. Begin by visiting Drosselgasse, a busy street noted for its traditional wine bars and entertainment.

Afternoon: Visit Siegfried's Mechanical Musical Instrument Museum and ride the cable car to the Niederwald Monument for breathtaking views of the Rhine Valley. Have lunch at one of the neighborhood cafes.

Evening: Go wine tasting at a nearby winery and eat a typical German supper. Return to Koblenz or spend the night in Rüdesheim if you like.

Four-Day Itinerary

Day 1 in Koblenz

Morning: Arrive and check in. Begin with a visit to Deutsches Eck and Ehrenbreitstein Fortress. Explore the surroundings and have lunch in the Old Town.

Afternoon: Tour the Church of Our Lady and the city's historical landmarks. Take a walk along the Rhine Promenade.

Evening: Take a Rhine River boat and dine at a local restaurant.

Day Two: Rüdesheim am Rhein.

Morning: Travel to Rüdesheim. Begin with a stroll to the Drosselgasse and a morning coffee.

Afternoon: Visit the Siegfried Mechanical Musical Instrument Museum. Take a cable car journey to the Niederwald Monument for spectacular views.

Evening: Enjoy supper at a local wine tavern and take in the scene.

Day Three: Bacharach and Boppard

Morning: Travel to Bacharach. Explore the old village and see Marksburg Castle.

Afternoon: Head to Boppard. Take a cable car trip for spectacular views and then wander along the river.

Evening: Return to Koblenz or remain the night in Boppard.

Day 4, Mainz

Morning: Travel to Mainz. Explore the ancient Old Town of Mainz and its Cathedral.

Afternoon: Take a stroll along the Rhine and explore local museums or galleries.

Evening: Have supper at a nearby restaurant and reflect on your journey.

Seven-Day Itinerary

Day 1-2 at Koblenz. Follow the two-day plan for Koblenz. Take extra time to explore the Old Town and visit the local eateries.

Day 3-4: Rüdesheim am Rhein - Explore Rüdesheim according to the 4-day schedule. Use the additional time to unwind and discover more of the town's hidden treasures and local attractions.

Day 5, Bacharach

Morning: Travel to Bacharach. Visit Marksburg Castle to see the town's historic beauty.

Afternoon: Have a leisurely lunch and walk around the town's picturesque streets.

nighttime: Spend the night in Bacharach and enjoy the town's nighttime vibe.

Day 6, Boppard

Morning: Travel to Boppard. Visit the Cable Car and take in the breathtaking scenery.

Afternoon: Take a leisurely walk along the river or browse local stores.

Evening: Have supper at a local restaurant and spend the night in Boppard.

Day 7, Mainz

Morning: Travel to Mainz. Explore the Old Town of Mainz and its Cathedral.

Afternoon: Explore local markets and museums. Enjoy lunch and final shopping.

Evening: Enjoy a goodbye supper and reflect on your journey before departing.

Tips for Customizing Your plan:

Flexibility: Adapt the plan to your interests and travel speed. Allow for additional time in locations you find particularly appealing.

Local ideas: To make your trip more enjoyable, seek out local ideas for meals and activities.

You may assure a satisfying and memorable trip to the Rhine Valley by carefully organizing your stay and adhering to these suggested itineraries. Whether you're on a quick trip or a longer adventure, the region has a fascinating combination of history, culture, and natural beauty to experience.

CHAPTER 8

PRACTICAL THINGS.

Traveling to the Rhine Valley may be a lovely experience, but understanding certain practical issues will help your vacation go more smoothly. This chapter provides critical information about currencies and payments, local traditions and etiquette, language and communication, and health and safety.

Currency and Payment

Currency

The Rhine Valley is located in Germany, and the Euro (€) is the national currency. The Euro is widely used throughout the European Union, making it a useful currency for regional visitors. As of the most recent prices, €1 is about similar to $1.10 USD, however exchange rates vary. It is a good idea to verify the current rate before departing.

Handling Money

ATMs: They are widely distributed across the Rhine Valley, including towns and cities. They are usually simple to discover in key areas and provide services in several languages. Be advised that some ATMs may impose a fee for overseas transactions.

Credit and debit cards are generally accepted across the Rhine Valley. The majority of hotels, restaurants, and stores accept major credit cards such as Visa, Mastercard, and American Express. However, some smaller shops, particularly in rural locations, may only accept cash.

Cash: It's a good idea to have some cash on hand for minor transactions or for visiting areas where credit cards aren't accepted. Euros may be exchanged in banks, exchange offices, and some hotels. Currency exchange services are also accessible in major airports and train stations.

Tipping is traditional in Germany, although it is not required. A tip of 5-10% is customary for good service in restaurants, however rounding up the amount is also popular. In pubs and cafés, it is customary to leave modest change.

Mobile Payments

Mobile payment solutions such as Apple Pay and Google Wallet are becoming increasingly popular in Germany, and they are widely accepted. Check with your bank or payment provider to check that your mobile payment option is compatible abroad.

Local Customs and Etiquette

Social Etiquette

Greetings: A handshake is the normal form of greeting in Germany, and it is customary to shake hands with everyone in the group when arriving or leaving. Maintain eye contact throughout the handshake.

Politeness: Germans prioritize punctuality and clear communication. Being on time for appointments and respecting personal space are essential. Polite terms like as "Bitte" (please) and "Danke" (thank you) are regularly employed.

Dining Etiquette: When dining out, it is traditional to wait until everyone has been served before beginning your meal. Keep your hands on the table (but not your elbows) and use utensils to eat most items. Tipping, as previously said, is expected but not excessive.

Cultural norms

Quiet Public areas: Germans place a high importance on tranquility in public areas such as public transit and restaurants. It is deemed disrespectful to speak loudly or disruptively.

Dress Code: Germans tend to dress stylishly and casually. More formal clothes is ideal for formal settings like dining at a high-end restaurant or attending an event. For informal events, nice and tidy casual attire is appropriate.

Rule Respect: Germans are well-known for following rules and regulations. Follow all local restrictions, including recycling standards, pedestrian guidelines, and traffic laws.

Dining out.

Reservations: It is recommended that you make a reservation in advance for popular restaurants, particularly those in tourist regions.

Ordering: When ordering meals, it is customary to wait for the waitress to approach you. In many instances, you will order at the counter rather than being served at the table.

Language & Communication

Language

The official language of Germany is German. While many Germans understand English, particularly in tourist destinations and big cities, it is polite to learn a few basic German words to improve your trip experience. Here are a few useful phrases.

Hello! Hello Goodbye: Please see you again.

Bitte: Thank you. Danke

Yes: Ja

No: Nein

Can you speak English? Do you speak English?

Communication Tips

English Speakers: In popular tourist sites like as Koblenz, Rüdesheim, and Heidelberg, many individuals in the hospitality business speak English. However, in smaller towns or rural regions, English may not be widely spoken, therefore a translation software might be useful.

Translation Apps: Apps such as Google Translate may be quite useful for overcoming language hurdles. Before your travel, download these applications and consider acquiring a local SIM card or confirming that your phone plan includes foreign data.

Emergency Assistance

Emergency Phone Number: In Germany, the fire, ambulance, and police services may be reached at 112.

Local Help: If you require assistance, do not hesitate to approach locals or the personnel at your lodging. Most folks will gladly assist you or lead you to the nearest tourist information office.

Health & Safety

Health precautions

Travel Insurance: It is strongly advised to have travel insurance that covers medical difficulties, accidents, and unexpected cancellations. Make sure your coverage covers overseas travel.

vaccines: While no particular vaccines are necessary for travel to Germany, standard immunizations such as measles, mumps, rubella, and influenza should be up to date.

medicine: If you require prescription medicine, bring it in its original packaging along with a copy of the prescription. If you have any special health concerns, you may want to bring a note from your doctor.

Healthcare System: Germany has a well developed healthcare system. In case of a medical emergency, go to the nearest hospital or clinic. Local pharmacists can also help with non-urgent medical situations.

Safety Tips

General Safety: Germany is typically safe for tourists. Petty crime, such as pickpocketing, can happen in busy areas, so keep your possessions safe and be aware of your surroundings.

Public Transportation: Public transportation is dependable and safe. However, be cautious about your personal things and avoid going alone late at night if feasible.

Local Laws: Familiarize oneself with local laws and customs to avoid any unintended legal consequences. For example, respecting driving regulations and refraining from public intoxication are vital.

Emergency Contacts:

Tourist Information facilities: Located in major towns and cities, these facilities provide local information, travel guidance, and emergency aid.

Consular Services: In the event of an emergency, such as a lost passport or legal concerns, contact your country's embassy or consulate. They can offer guidance and support.

Understanding these practical features of Rhine Valley tourism can help you explore the region with ease and enjoy your time. Currency management, local traditions, language abilities, and health measures all help to ensure a successful and pleasurable vacation.

CHAPTER 9

TRANSPORTATION IN THE RHINE VALLEY

The Rhine Valley has a choice of transportation alternatives to let you enjoy its breathtaking scenery and lovely villages. Whether you prefer public transportation, driving, cycling, or another mode, knowing your options will improve your experience and make travel within the region more convenient. In this chapter, we will look at the main modes of transportation accessible in the Rhine Valley.

Public Transportation.

Overview

The Rhine Valley's public transportation system is well-developed, with dependable and efficient choices for traveling between cities, villages, and tourist destinations. The network comprises trains, buses, and ferries, making it simple to explore the region without a personal automobile.

Trains

Regional Trains: The Rhine Valley is served by the Deutsche Bahn (DB) network, which runs regular regional trains linking major cities and towns. For example, the Rhine-Ruhr Express (RRX) and regional trains like as the RB (Regionalbahn) and RE (Regional Express) may transport you to famous places like Koblenz, Mainz, and Rüdesheim.

Scenic lines: The Rhine Valley is known for its attractive rail lines. The Rhine Valley Railway (Rheinbahn) provides magnificent trips along the river with breathtaking vistas of castles, vineyards, and attractive villages. One of the most gorgeous roads is the Mittelrheinbahn, which connects Bingen and Koblenz and is recognized for its stunning scenery and historic monuments.

Buses

Local Buses: Local bus services supplement train travel by linking small towns and rural areas that are not immediately served by rail. These buses are operated by a variety of regional businesses and are frequently coordinated with rail timetables to guarantee smooth connections.

Regional bus lines connect bigger towns and tourism spots in the Rhine Valley. They provide routes that link with rail stations and allow access to sights that are not easily accessible by train.

Ferries

Rhine River Ferries: The Rhine River is an important transit corridor. Passenger and automobile boats run along the river, providing a unique and picturesque route linking cities on opposing sides. Ferries are particularly popular for crossings between Bacharach and Kaub, as well as between St. Goar and St. Goarshausen.

tourist Cruises: For a relaxing excursion, tourist cruises on the Rhine River are available. These cruises frequently feature guided tours and stops at significant locations, resulting in a relaxed and educational vacation experience.

Tickets and Passes

Single Tickets: Tickets for public transportation can be purchased at train stations, bus stops, or online through the Deutsche Bahn website or App. Prices vary depending on the distance and kind of service.

Day Passes: Day passes provide unrestricted travel within a specific time period. These might be useful for travelers who want to utilize public transportation frequently in a single day.

Regional Passes: The Rheinland-Pfalz Ticket provides one day of unrestricted travel on regional trains and buses within the state of Rhineland-Palatinate. This package is suitable for visitors who want to visit various towns in the area.

Car Rental

Overview

Renting a car allows you to explore the Rhine Valley at your own speed. Driving, with its well-maintained highways and picturesque pathways, is a popular choice for people who want to see less accessible locations or travel on their own timetable.

Rental agencies

Major Rental Companies: International and local automobile rental businesses are available in major cities such as Koblenz, Mainz, and Wiesbaden, as well as airports and rail stations. Hertz, Avis, Europcar, and Sixt provide a wide choice of automobiles to meet a variety of demands.

Booking: It is recommended that you reserve your rental car ahead of time, especially during busy tourist seasons. Online booking systems and rental agency websites allow you to compare costs and reserve automobiles.

Driving Conditions:

Roads: The Rhine Valley has a well-developed road network, including highways (Autobahnen) that connect large cities and beautiful routes along the Rhine River. Secondary highways and rural lanes connect smaller towns and attractions.

Traffic: Most traffic is acceptable, but keep an eye out during peak hours in bigger cities. Parking may be restricted in busy tourist destinations, so plan accordingly.

Parking rules vary by town. Pay attention to parking zone signs and use public parking when available. Parking in ancient towns may be limited to specific locations, so plan on walking from your assigned parking place to your final destination.

Driving Tips:

Speed restrictions: Follow speed restrictions, which are typically 50 km/h (31 mph) in urban areas, 100 km/h (62 mph) on rural roads, and 130 km/h (81 mph) on highways, unless otherwise specified.

Road Signs: Learn the German road signs and traffic standards. For example, roundabouts are widespread, and right-of-way requirements must be respected.

Cycling and Walking

Cycling

Bike lanes: The Rhine Valley has numerous and well-marked bike lanes, making it a popular destination for cyclists. The Rhine Cycle Route (Rheinradweg) runs along the river from the Swiss border to the North Sea, offering a lovely and relaxing ride through vineyards, woods, and ancient cities.

Bike Rentals: Many villages and cities along the Rhine provide bicycle rental services. Rental stores provide a wide range of bikes, including regular cycles, e-bikes, and mountain bikes. Some bike rental organizations also offer guided trips.

Cycling Tips: where cycling, be cautious of traffic restrictions and use designated bike routes where available. Helmets are optional but suggested for safety. Before heading out, inspect your bike and keep a repair kit on hand for small concerns.

Walking

Walking Tours: The Rhine Valley's ancient cities and attractive scenery are best explored on foot. Many communities provide guided walking tours that highlight major features and provide historical context.

Hiking paths: The Rhine Valley has a number of hiking paths for people who enjoy more difficult activities. The Rheinsteig and Rheinburgenweg are famous routes that provide breathtaking vistas while passing past old castles and ruins.

Town Exploration: By walking around towns like Bacharach, Rüdesheim, and Heidelberg, you can fully appreciate their charm and architectural splendor. Many towns feature pedestrian zones where automobiles are not permitted, making it convenient and safe to explore on foot.

Taxis and Ridesharing

Taxis

Availability: Taxis are widely available in major towns and cities. They may be hailed on the street, located at designated taxi stops, or booked over the phone. Taxi services are typically dependable and provide a convenient way to move around when public transportation is limited.

rates: Taxi rates are metered, and costs vary according on distance and time of day. There may be additional fees for baggage or transit outside the municipal boundaries. Before embarking on your journey, it is advisable to confirm the costs with the driver.

Booking: Most cabs may be reserved through local taxi firms or smartphone applications. In locations like as Mainz and Koblenz, taxi firms frequently offer dedicated apps for simpler booking.

Ride-Sharing

Services: Ride-sharing services such as Uber and Lyft are gaining popularity across Germany, especially the Rhine Valley. These services provide an alternative to typical taxis and can be useful for point-to-point transportation.

Availability: Ride-sharing services may be more common in major cities and metropolitan regions. Availability in small towns or rural locations may be restricted.

App Usage: To utilize ride-sharing services, download the appropriate app (such as Uber) and establish an account. The app will let you order trips, follow your driver, and pay electronically.

The Rhine Valley is easy to navigate, thanks to the numerous transit alternatives available. Whether you want to tour by rail, automobile, bicycle, or foot, each way provides distinct benefits and possibilities to discover this lovely region. Understanding your alternatives and planning ahead of time will result in a stress-free and pleasurable trip.

CHAPTER 10

DINING AND CUISINE

Exploring the Rhine Valley is more than simply seeing the beautiful scenery and historical sites; it's also about learning about the region's culinary traditions. The region has a fantastic selection of eating alternatives, ranging from classic German food to new culinary experiences. In this chapter, we will look at classic Rhine Valley meals, propose excellent restaurants and cafés, and highlight local food markets where you may sample the region's flavors firsthand.

Traditional Rhine Valley Dishes.

Rheinischer Sauerbraten

Rheinischer Sauerbraten, a traditional Rhine Valley cuisine, is a sort of pot roast that is marinated in vinegar, red wine, and spices for many days before being slow-cooked until tender. This substantial dish is usually served with red cabbage, dumplings, and a thick sauce. The marinade gives a tangy flavor that complements the meat's savory overtones, making it popular with both residents and visitors.

Reibekuchen (potato pancakes)

Potato pancakes, often known as reibekuchen, are a popular Rhine Valley dessert. These crispy, golden-brown pancakes are produced by combining grated potatoes, onions, eggs, and flour, then frying until crisp. They are typically served with applesauce or sour cream and can be eaten as a snack or as part of a meal. During the holidays, you may find Reibekuchen in local Christmas markets, where they are very popular.

Himmel und Erde

Himmel und Erde, or "Heaven and Earth," is a traditional meal that mixes mashed potatoes ("earth") with apple sauce ("heaven"). This simple yet substantial dish is frequently served with sausages or black pudding. The sweet and salty mix of apples and potatoes results in a soothing and tasty dish that embodies the region's down-to-earth cuisine.

Weißwurst (white sausages)

Weißwurst are delicate sausages prepared from minced veal and pig and seasoned with parsley, lemon zest, and spices. They originated in Bavaria but are popular in the Rhine Valley. They're generally served with sweet mustard and pretzels. The sausages are steamed rather than grilled or fried, producing a soft and mild taste.

Rheinischer Apfelkuchen (Rhenish Apple Cake).

For dessert, Rheinischer Apfelkuchen is a must-have. This apple cake has a buttery crust filled with thinly sliced apples, cinnamon, and sugar. The end product is a rich, moist cake with the ideal blend of sweet and sour tastes. It's commonly served with whipped cream or a scoop of vanilla ice cream.

Käsefondue

Käsefondue, while traditionally linked with Swiss cuisine, has found a place in the Rhine Valley's culinary repertoire, particularly during the winter months. This meal consists of melting a variety of cheeses, including Gruyère and Emmental, with white wine and garlic. Diners use long forks to dip chunks of crusty bread into the gooey cheese concoction. It's a communal meal that's ideal for sharing and enjoying with friends and family.

Wine and Beer Pairings

The Rhine Valley is known for its vineyards, which produce superb Riesling and other white wines. Local wines are frequently served alongside regional foods, complementing the tastes of both. Similarly, classic German beers, such as Pilsners and Weizens, go well with heavy meals and are a cornerstone of local eating culture.

Recommended Restaurants and Cafés

Restaurant zum Goldenen Schaf

Restaurant Zum Goldenen Schaf, located in Bacharach, provides a lovely dining experience including traditional Rhine Valley food. The menu includes traditional meals such as Rheinischer Sauerbraten and Reibekuchen, made with fresh, local ingredients. The comfortable, rustic environment, replete with wooden beams and a pleasant ambiance, makes it ideal for a relaxing supper.

Winehaus Neuner

Weinhaus Neuner, located in Rüdesheim, is well-known for its large wine selection and regional delicacies. The restaurant's menu features a wide range of meals, from light appetizers to hefty mains like Himmel und Erde. The educated staff is glad to recommend wines that go well with your meal, and the outside sitting area provides wonderful views of the Rhine River.

Beautiful life

Schönes Leben in Mainz is a great place to try a more contemporary take on Rhine Valley food. This restaurant has a distinctive menu that combines classic German tastes with modern technology. Dishes such as Weißwurst are gourmetized, and the restaurant's modern décor and casual environment make it a favorite hangout for both residents and visitors.

Café Restaurant Brückenblick

Café-Restaurant Brückenblick, located in Koblenz, offers stunning views of the Rhine River and the historic Deutsche Eck. The café serves a variety of items, from light snacks and pastries to more substantial meals. It's an excellent area for sipping a coffee or tea while admiring the gorgeous surroundings.

Cafe Extrablatt

Café Extrablatt, a well-known brand with a presence in Wiesbaden, offers a relaxed and welcoming atmosphere for breakfast, brunch, and lunch. The menu combines classic German meals with foreign selections, making it ideal for a relaxing lunch at any time of day.

The large assortment of cakes and pastries is ideal for a sweet treat.

Restaurant Johann Lafer

Restaurant Johann Lafer in the lovely village of Leutesdorf is well-known for its fine dining experience. The restaurant's menu emphasizes fresh ingredients and provides a fine dining twist on regional cuisine. With its gorgeous setting and great service, it's a wonderful choice for a special event or a lavish supper.

Winehaus Stöhr

Weinhaus Stöhr, a family-owned restaurant in Bad Salzig, is well-known for its friendly hospitality and traditional meals. The cuisine includes local classics like Käsefondue and Rheinischer Apfelkuchen. The restaurant's vast wine list includes options from local wineries, which enhances the dining experience.

Local Food Markets.

Koblenz Market

The Koblenz Market, located in the town's center square, is a lively spot to sample local cuisine and buy for fresh vegetables. Vendors sell cheeses, meats, baked foods, and unique things. The market is most popular during the spring and summer months, when it's a perfect place to pick up picnic items or experience local specialties.

Mainz Farmers Market

The Mainz Farmers' Market, located on the Schillerplatz, is a thriving hive of activity where you can discover high-quality local products. The market has vendors offering fruits, vegetables, specialty cheeses, breads, and other items. It's a great place to try regional delicacies and get fresh supplies for home cooking.

Rüdesheim's Christmas Market

The Rüdesheim Christmas Market is a spectacular event hosted in the town's historic center over the holidays. It has a number of kiosks selling festive dishes, such as classic German sausages, mulled wine, and sweet sweets like Lebkuchen (gingerbread). The market's attractive ambiance, replete with dazzling lights and festive decorations, makes it a must-see for everyone visiting the Rhine Valley during the winter season.

Bacharach Market

The Bacharach Market, nestled against the background of this charming village, provides a delectable assortment of local produce. From fresh fruits and vegetables to artisan crafts and local wines, the market offers a glimpse into Rhine Valley life. It's a terrific location to meet people and discover unique regional items.

Heidelberg Market

The Heidelberg Market, located in the Altstadt (Old Town), is a bustling place to sample local dishes and enjoy the lively ambiance. The market has a variety of exhibitors that sell anything from fresh fruit to gourmet meals. It's an excellent place to sample regional cuisine while also immersing yourself in Heidelberg's history.

Wiesbaden Market

Wiesbaden's Market on the Schlossplatz is a popular spot for fresh vegetables, baked foods, and specialized items. The market is open year-round, with a regular mix of local goods and seasonal items. It's a terrific spot to sample the Rhine Valley's gastronomic diversity while also taking a leisurely stroll among the market stalls.

The Rhine Valley's eating scene has something for everyone, from traditional dishes honoring the region's rich culinary heritage to trendy eateries and lively food markets. By sampling local dishes, visiting recommended restaurants, and touring bustling markets, you'll obtain a better understanding of the tastes that distinguish this lovely area.

CHAPTER 11

SHOPPING.

The Rhine Valley is not only a visual and culinary delight, but also a thriving retail destination. From beautiful village markets to high-end stores, the area provides a diversified shopping experience. Whether you're looking for one-of-a-kind souvenirs, local specialties, or a relaxing shopping experience, the Rhine Valley offers something for you. In this chapter, we'll look at the greatest souvenir and gift possibilities, highlight significant local markets and stores, and walk you through the region's most popular shopping areas.

Souvenirs & Gifts

Traditional Rhine Valley souvenirs

When it comes to souvenirs, the Rhine Valley has a wide selection of distinctive and unforgettable goods that express the soul of the region.

Some popular alternatives are:

Wine and beer: The Rhine Valley is known for its high-quality wines, notably Riesling. A bottle of local wine is an ideal keepsake. Traditional German beers, frequently brewed by local brewers, are also available, making them ideal for sharing a taste of the region with loved ones back home.

Handcrafted Goods: Look for handmade products such as wooden carvings, classic German beer steins, and delicate glassware. These one-of-a-kind objects, created by a variety of local craftspeople, are excellent souvenirs or presents.

Cuckoo Clocks: Although they originated in the Black Forest region, cuckoo clocks are popular across Germany and serve as a beautiful remembrance of your visit. These finely made clocks are frequently embellished with classical patterns and make ideal gifts or souvenirs.

Pottery and Ceramics: Local pottery and ceramics, which are frequently ornamented with traditional patterns or regional sceneries, are another good option. Mugs, plates, and vases are examples of useful items that also showcase local artistry.

Local Delicacies: Regional specialties such as Rheinischer Apfelkuchen (apple cake) mix and traditional German chocolates can be wrapped for presents. They provide as a delicious recall of the tastes of the Rhine Valley.

classic attire: Consider purchasing some classic German attire, such as a Bavarian hat or dirndl. These clothes are frequently embellished with regional needlework and can be treasured as a one-of-a-kind souvenir.

Where to Find Unique Souvenirs?

Local Artisan stores: In places such as Bacharach and Rüdesheim, small stores and boutiques frequently sell handcrafted products manufactured by local craftsmen. These businesses are ideal for obtaining unique items.

Wine and Beer stores: Specialized stores in locations like Koblenz and Mainz sell a broad variety of local wines and beers. These establishments frequently have experienced staff who can assist you in selecting the ideal bottle to take home.

Markets and Fairs: Local markets and fairs, notably Christmas markets, are good places to buy mementos. Vendors at these events frequently sell homemade items and regional specialties.

Local Markets and Shops.

Bacharach Market

Bacharach's market, located in the lovely town center, provides a great selection of local items. The market's vendors provide fresh vegetables, specialty delicacies, and handcrafted crafts. Local cheeses and cured meats are available, as well as one-of-a-kind artisan products. It's an excellent spot to sample regional cuisines and pick up a unique keepsake.

Koblenz Market

The Koblenz Market is a lively facility located in the city's main plaza. This market is noted for its broad selection of items, which includes local vegetables, gourmet cuisine, and regional crafts. It's the perfect place to acquire fresh ingredients for a picnic or unusual presents to take home. The market's bustling environment enhances the shopping experience.

Mainz Farmers Market

The Mainz Farmers' Market, located on Schillerplatz, is a thriving center of activity. It has a number of vendors selling seasonal fruits and vegetables, specialty cheeses, and freshly baked products. The market is a good opportunity to try local cuisines and purchase fresh vegetables. It's also an excellent opportunity to meet local merchants and learn more about the area's culinary heritage.

Rüdesheim's Christmas Market

The Rüdesheim Christmas Market, located in the picturesque town center, transforms into a spectacular fantasy throughout the holiday season. The market has several vendors offering Christmas ornaments, crafts, and seasonal refreshments. It's a lovely spot to discover one-of-a-kind presents and indulge in traditional holiday delights.

Heidelberg Market

The Heidelberg Market, in the center of the city's Old Town, sells a variety of fresh fruit, gourmet cuisine, and local crafts. It's a busy and bustling market where you can sample regional delicacies and buy for unusual things. The market's location in a historic city adds to its appeal.

Wiesbaden Market

Wiesbaden's Market on Schlossplatz is a popular spot for both locals and tourists. It sells a broad variety of items, including fresh fruit, baked foods, handmade crafts, and souvenirs. The market's wide offers and friendly ambiance make it a fun location to explore and purchase.

Shopping Districts.

Koblenz Shopping District

Koblenz provides a bustling shopping experience with its broad selection of stores and boutiques. The core shopping district surrounding Löhrstraße is home to a variety of retail outlets, including fashion boutiques, jewelry shops, and specialized stores. You may also visit the Forum Mittelrhein, a contemporary shopping mall that has popular retail companies and a range of food alternatives. Shopping in Koblenz is made even more appealing by its closeness to the Rhine River.

Heidelberg Altstadt (Old Town).

Heidelberg's Altstadt is a lovely neighborhood with small lanes, old houses, and a mix of boutique shops and bigger retail establishments. The Hauptstraße is the major shopping route, lined with a wide range of retailers, from high-end designer boutiques to one-of-a-kind specialized shops. The neighborhood also has nice cafés and quaint stores where you may purchase regional items.

Mainz City Center

Mainz's city center has a vibrant shopping atmosphere with a mix of modern and historic retail businesses. Breidenbacherstraße and Ludwigsstraße are prominent shopping streets, including both foreign and local stores. Mainz also has various retail arcades and malls, which offer a variety of shopping alternatives in a convenient location.

Wiesbaden Wilhelmstraße

Wiesbaden's main retail route, Wilhelmstraße, is recognized for its luxury shops and high-end businesses. The neighborhood is home to a variety of fashion, jewelry, and gourmet food outlets. The street's exquisite architecture and closeness to historic attractions make it an appealing location for shopping and wandering.

Rüdesheim Shopping

In Rüdesheim, the shopping experience revolves around the picturesque town center and Drosselgasse. This neighborhood is noted for its small stores that sell local crafts, souvenirs, and regional items. It's an excellent spot to locate one-of-a-kind items and relax while shopping in a beautiful atmosphere.

Bacharach Shopping

Bacharach's commercial sector is distinguished by its tiny, independent stores and local artisan boutiques. The town center is home to a variety of shops selling homemade crafts, local specialties, and souvenirs. Bacharach's small environment and historic charm make shopping a memorable and delightful experience.

The Rhine Valley provides a diverse shopping experience with something for everyone's taste and interests. From beautiful local markets and artisanal stores to bustling retail districts, the region offers several options to find unique gifts, experience regional specialties, and go on a fun shopping spree. Whether you're seeking for a unique present, local delicacies, or just to explore the local retail scene, the Rhine Valley's shopping selections will not disappoint.

CHAPTER 12

NIGHTLIFE & ENTERTAINMENT

The Rhine Valley is more than simply a scenic destination during the day; it also has a thriving nightlife and entertainment scene once the sun goes down. From bustling pubs and clubs to engaging live music performances and culturally rich festivals, the area provides a wide range of nighttime entertainment alternatives. In this chapter, we'll look at the top pubs and clubs, live music and performance places, and the cultural events and festivals that make Rhine Valley nightlife so unique.

Bars and clubs.

Koblenz: Trendy and Classic Favorites.

Koblenz, a lively city at the junction of the Rhine and Moselle rivers, has a vibrant nightlife scene. The Altstadt (Old Town) has several pubs and clubs that appeal to a variety of tastes:

Brauhaus Koblenz: A typical beer hall that serves a variety of local and regional beers. The vibrant environment is supplemented by traditional German pub cuisine and occasional live music. It's an excellent place to learn about local beer culture in a friendly atmosphere.

Dreikönigskeller: With its pleasant setting and comprehensive beverage menu, Dreikönigskeller attracts a diverse clientele. The bar is well-known for its inventive cocktails and laid-back environment, making it ideal for both casual hangouts and smaller events.

Club 101: For those seeking to dance the night away, Club 101 offers a lively partying atmosphere with DJ performances from a variety of genres. It's a popular choice for young people and night owls looking for a high-energy atmosphere.

Heidelberg combines historic charm and modern vibes.

Heidelberg, renowned for its romantic attractiveness and historical setting, has a mix of classic and contemporary nightlife options:

Kulturbrauerei Heidelberg: A brewpub housed in a historic structure that serves a variety of craft beers made on-site. The facility hosts live music events and attracts a varied mix of customers, resulting in a dynamic and stimulating environment.

Harlem pub: This trendy pub is recognized for its inventive drinks and elegant atmosphere. It's a popular place to spend an elegant evening, with a selection of gourmet bar snacks.

Club Nachtwerk: Located in the center of Heidelberg, Nachtwerk is a high-energy nightclub with an amazing lineup of DJs and themed events. It's a popular choice for anyone wishing to experience the city's bustling dance culture.

Mainz: A Center of Entertainment

Mainz's nightlife culture is broad, ranging from bustling pubs to trendy cocktail bars:

Goldener Engel: This classic bar is known for its diverse beer variety and welcoming environment. It's the perfect spot to spend a relaxing evening with friends, replete with substantial German meals.

Exil, a prominent nightclub in Mainz, provides a variety of themed parties and DJ events. The club's vibrant atmosphere and amazing sound system make it a popular destination for people wishing to dance and mingle.

Kaffeemühle: An unusual location that mixes a café environment with live music performances. Kaffeemühle is ideal for a relaxing evening spent listening to acoustic concerts or jazz performances.

Live Music & Performances

Koblenz has a mix of local talent and touring acts.

Koblenz's live music scene features a diverse range of genres and settings:

Lahnaue: A prominent live music venue, Lahnaue showcases a variety of concerts, including local bands and international artists. The tiny location allows for a close-up encounter with the music, making it a popular choice among music fans.

Rhens Kulturzentrum: The cultural center regularly hosts live music events, such as classical concerts, jazz performances, and folk music. The center's extensive programming appeals to a wide variety of musical inclinations.

Heidelberg: Music in a Historic Setting.

Heidelberg's rich cultural past offers various alternatives for live music and performances:

Heidelberger Stadthalle: A popular venue for concerts and classical performances, the Stadthalle accommodates a wide range of events, including symphonic concerts and solo recitals. The attractive location and superb acoustics improve the musical experience.

Sommertheater Heidelberg: For individuals interested in theater and performance art, the Sommertheater presents a variety of theatrical shows, ranging from classic plays to current pieces. Outdoor performances in the summer give a certain touch to the experience.

Mainz: A cultural melting pot.

Mainz has numerous locations that provide live music and performances:

Staatstheater Mainz: This famous theater presents a varied program of opera, ballet, and drama. The theater's shows are well-known for their excellent quality and creative excellence, making it a cultural highlight of your stay.

Club Stereo: A prominent live music venue, Club Stereo hosts local bands, new musicians, and sometimes international acts. The venue's compact ambiance makes it ideal for discovering new music and enjoying a dynamic performance.

Cultural Activities and Festivals

Koblenz celebrates throughout the year.

Koblenz holds a range of cultural events and festivals that represent the city's active communal life.

Koblenz Christmas Market: Located in the historic centre, this festive market is a hallmark of the holiday season. Visitors may enjoy traditional Christmas snacks, handcrafted items, and live entertainment in a beautifully adorned environment.

Rhein in Flammen (Rhine in Flames): This stunning event, held yearly along the Rhine River, features a massive fireworks show synced to music. It's one of the region's most popular events, with attendees traveling from all around Germany and beyond.

Heidelberg: A Center for Cultural Events

Heidelberg's cultural calendar is full of events that honor the city's artistic and historical heritage:

Heidelberger Frühling (Heidelberg Spring event): This prestigious music event comprises performances by world-class classical soloists and orchestras. The festival draws a global audience and takes place in a variety of historic buildings around the city.

Heidelberg Castle Festival: This yearly festival, held against the breathtaking background of Heidelberg Castle, features a variety of performances such as opera, theater, and concerts. The historical setting gives a dramatic element to the performances.

Mainz: The City of Festivals

Mainz has a diverse range of festivals that represent its vibrant cultural scene:

Mainzer Fastnacht (Mainz Carnival) is one of Germany's largest and most well-known carnival festivals, with colorful parades, vibrant street parties, and traditional music. The festival, held every February, is a highlight of the city's cultural calendar.

Mainz Wine Market: This festival showcases the region's rich winemaking legacy through tastings, wine-related activities, and live entertainment. The market draws wine connoisseurs and provides an opportunity to taste local vintages in a festive setting.

The Rhine Valley's nightlife and entertainment scene has something for everyone, including busy pubs and clubs, exciting live music, and cultural events. Whether you want to go out for a night on the town, experience the region's dynamic music scene, or participate in one-of-a-kind cultural festivals, the Rhine Valley has a broad and fascinating selection of alternatives to make your visit more enjoyable.

CHAPTER 13

OUTDOOR ACTIVITIES.

The Rhine Valley provides an unparalleled selection of outdoor activities for nature lovers, adventurers, and those who simply want to enjoy the breathtaking scenery. Whether you enjoy hiking paths, river cruises, bicycle routes, or visiting natural reserves and parks, the region has plenty of possibilities to interact with the great outdoors. This chapter will walk you through the greatest outdoor adventures that the Rhine Valley has to offer.

Hiking Trails.

The Rhine Valley is known for its beautiful hiking paths that wind through lush woods, vineyards, and lovely riverbanks.

Here are some of the most prominent paths with varied degrees of difficulty and beautiful views:

The Rheinsteig Trail:

Overview: The Rheinsteig Trail, which spans 320 kilometers from Bonn to Wiesbaden, is one of Germany's most recognized long-distance hiking paths. It follows the Rhine River, offering breathtaking views of the river, castles, and picturesque villages along the route.

Highlights include the trail across the Middle Rhine Valley, which is noted for its stunning cliffs and old castles like Marksburg and Rheinfels. The path also leads hikers through the lovely towns of Bacharach and Boppard.

Difficulty varies based on the section. The full path may be completed in 15-20 days, although shorter day treks are also an option.

The Rheinburgenweg Trail:

Overview: This 200-kilometer track connects Bingen and Bonn, traversing through the Rhine Gorge, a UNESCO World Heritage Site. It features a mix of river vistas and rough terrain.

Highlights: Hikers will see several castles, vineyards, and attractive villages. The Drachenfels (Dragon's Rock) and Rüdesheim are two must-see destinations.

Difficulty is moderate, with some steep portions. The track is well-marked, making it suitable for both experienced hikers and beginners.

Pfalzer Trail:

Overview: The Pfalz Trail winds through the Palatinate Forest, providing a peaceful respite from the bustling Rhine Valley. It has a range of sceneries, such as woods, meadows, and panoramic views.

Highlights: The walk passes numerous magnificent sites, including Kalmit Peak, which offers panoramic views of the Rhine Plain. The path also travels through lovely villages and historical landmarks.

Difficulty is moderate, with well-kept trails and good signage. Suitable for people seeking a less strenuous walk.

Loreley trail:

Overview: This walk is focused on the Lorelei Rock, one of the Rhine Valley's most iconic sights. It provides an immersive hiking experience with breathtaking vistas.

Highlights: The walk offers panoramic views of the Rhine River and the stunning cliffs of Lorelei Rock. Hikers may explore the surrounding woodland and appreciate the natural beauty of the region.

Difficulty: Easy to moderate, with gradual inclines and clearly designated trails.

river cruises.

Exploring the Rhine Valley from the river provides a unique perspective on the area's natural beauty and historical landmarks. River cruises provide a relaxing way to explore the Rhine River, with options ranging from short trips to multi-day voyages.

Scenic Rhine River Cruises:

Overview: Scenic Rhine River Cruises provide a relaxing and pleasant way to see the Rhine Valley. These cruises often feature guided excursions, onboard facilities, and stops at notable riverside spots.

Highlights: Passengers may see renowned locations like the Lorelei Rock, historic castles, and picturesque towns like Bacharach and Rüdesheim. Many cruises feature trips to local vineyards and historical places.

Types: Day cruises run a few hours, while multi-day excursions cover a large stretch of the Rhine River. Some ships also have specialty itineraries, such as wine tours or historical excursions.

Wine Cruise:

Overview: Wine cruises are a popular way to explore the Rhine Valley's well-known vineyards and wineries. These cruises frequently incorporate wine tastings and vineyard excursions as part of the program.

Highlights: Visitors may explore well-known wine-producing villages like Rüdesheim and Bingen, sample local wines, and learn about the winemaking process. Many wine cruises feature excursions to old castles and quaint towns.

Types: Wine cruises are usually offered as part of longer Rhine River cruises or as standalone wine-themed excursions.

Private Boat Rental:

Overview: For a more customized experience, travelers may rent private boats and explore the Rhine River at their leisure. This option offers flexibility and the ability to construct a personalized itinerary.

Highlights: Renting a boat allows you to explore less-accessible regions of the river and enjoy peaceful, gorgeous settings. It's an excellent place to spend a picnic on the river or simply relax and take in the scenery.

Types: Depending on your party size and requirements, you may rent anything from a small motorboat to a huge yacht.

Cycle Routes

The Rhine Valley has a variety of bicycle routes that appeal to different skill levels and interests. Whether you're a novice cyclist or an expert rider, there's a route for you.

Rhine Cycling Route (Rheinradweg):

Overview: The Rhine Cycle Route is a well-established trail that follows the Rhine River from the Swiss border to the North Sea. The route across the Rhine Valley is extremely picturesque, with vistas of vineyards, castles, and attractive villages.

Highlights: Cyclists will see historic sights like the Lorelei Rock, the Rhine Gorge, and other attractive villages. The route includes major cycling sites such as Rüdesheim and Koblenz.

Difficulty level: Easy to moderate, with primarily flat stretches along the river and some gently sloping terrain. Suitable for cyclists of all abilities.

Mosel Bicycle Route:

Overview: Although this route mostly follows the Moselle River, it meets with the Rhine Valley around Koblenz and provides a picturesque alternative to the Rhine Cycle Route.

Highlights: The Mosel Cycle Route has stunning vineyards, medieval villages, and majestic castles. It's a terrific way to explore the Moselle River while being close to the Rhine.

Difficulty: Easy to moderate, with primarily flat terrain and a few minor inclines.

Palatinate Forest Cycling Route:

Overview: This route leads cyclists through the Palatinate Forest, offering a unique viewpoint on the Rhine Valley's natural splendor. It boasts woodland pathways, stunning views, and attractive settlements.

Highlights: Cyclists will appreciate the calm of the forest, charming villages, and magnificent overlooks. The road is less traveled, providing a tranquil riding experience.

Difficulty: Moderate, including some uphill stretches along woodland paths. Suitable for intermediate to advanced bikers.

Rhine Gorge Bicycle Route:

Overview: This specialty route concentrates on the breathtaking Rhine Gorge, a UNESCO World Heritage Site. It provides a more strenuous ride with steep hills and great scenery.

Highlights: The route takes riders into the heart of the Rhine Gorge, providing up-close views of the sheer cliffs, castles, and vineyards. It's an excellent way to explore the gorge's distinctive environment.

Difficulty: Challenging, including steep climbs and descents. Recommended for experienced riders looking for a more challenging trip.

Natural Reserves and Parks

The Rhine Valley is home to various natural reserves and parks, providing possibilities for outdoor adventure and wildlife observation. These protected areas highlight the region's varied ecosystems and natural beauty.

Rheinauen Natural Reserve:

Overview: The Rheinauen Nature Reserve, located near Bonn, is a huge wetland region that serves as significant habitat for a variety of bird species and fauna. It's an excellent spot for birding and admiring the natural scenery.

Highlights: The reserve has walking routes, observation platforms, and information explaining the area flora and wildlife. It's a tranquil setting for trekking and wildlife photography.

Activities include bird viewing, hiking, and nature photography. Guided tours and educational events are frequently provided.

Palatinate Forest Nature Park:

Overview: This huge natural park spans 1,700 square kilometers and has a variety of landforms, including woods, meadows, and hills. It is a popular site for hiking, cycling, and other outdoor activities.

Highlights: The park has several paths, picturesque overlooks, and opportunities to see animals. It also has various historical sites and cultural landmarks.

Activities include hiking, cycling, animal observation, and visiting historical places. The park provides a variety of themed paths and guided excursions.

The Siebengebirge Nature Park

Overview: The Siebengebirge Nature Park, located near Bonn, is recognized for its unique peaks and diverse wildlife. The park provides a variety of outdoor activities and magnificent perspectives.

Highlights: The park is home to the famous Drachenfels (Dragon's Rock) and a number of other notable peaks. It's an excellent area for hiking, with routes that provide panoramic views of the Rhine River and surrounding scenery.

Activities include hiking, nature hikes, and enjoying breathtaking views. The park also provides educational programs on its natural and cultural history.

The Hunsrück-Hochwald National Park

Overview: Located west of the Rhine Valley, this national park boasts a broad range of landscapes, including thick woods, undulating hills, and river valleys. It's an excellent choice for outdoor enthusiasts seeking seclusion and natural beauty.

Highlights: The park has various well-marked paths, including those through old woods and along lovely rivers. It is also recognized for its abundant fauna, which includes deer and a variety of bird species.

Activities: Hiking and animal watching and explore natural sceneries. The park provides guided tours and educational programs on its ecosystems.

The Rhine Valley's outdoor activities cater to a diverse variety of interests and skill sets. Whether you're hiking along gorgeous paths, boating the Rhine River, cycling through picturesque landscapes, or visiting nature reserves, the region provides several possibilities to connect with nature and appreciate its beauty. This varied range of activities assures that any outdoor enthusiast may find something to fit their tastes and make memorable experiences in this breathtaking region of the globe.

CHAPTER 14

FAMILY-FRIENDLY ACTIVITIES.

Traveling with children necessitates some preparation to guarantee that everyone in the family has an enjoyable experience. The Rhine Valley, with its blend of historical charm and natural beauty, provides a variety of family-friendly activities. From fascinating attractions to family-friendly eating options and educational activities, this chapter will walk you through the best ways to keep your family interested and involved during your vacation.

Attractions for Children

The Rhine Valley is full of sights that will captivate the imaginations of young vacationers.

Here are some of the best places that cater particularly to children, delivering fun and excitement for all ages:

Loreley Rock and Visitors' Center:

Location: St. Goarshausen, Germany.

Overview: The Loreley Rock is a well-known landmark that offers breathtaking views of the Rhine River and surrounding region. The Visitor Center includes interactive displays and multimedia presentations about the Loreley tale and Rhine history.

Highlights for Children: The visitor center's exhibits feature interactive displays and a multimedia presentation that presents the Loreley myth in an appealing manner. Kids may also enjoy the magnificent views and hike the nearby trails.

Family Tip: The location is suitable for families with small children, and there are several picnic sites where you can enjoy a family dinner with a view.

Phantasialand Theme Park:

Location: Brühl, Germany.

Overview: Phantasialand is a vast theme park that offers a range of rides and activities for children and families. The park is separated into themed regions, each offering a unique experience, ranging from exhilarating rides to family-friendly performances.

Highlights for Children: Attractions include roller coasters, themed attractions such as the "Temple of the Nighthawk," and water rides. There are other places designated for smaller children, such as "Wuze Town" and "Fantasy Land."

Family Tips: The park provides family-friendly features such as stroller rentals and children's meals at several eateries. Check the park's schedule for upcoming concerts and parades.

Rheinpark, Koblenz:

Location: Koblenz, Germany.

Overview: Rheinpark is a big public park on the Rhine River that provides plenty of green space and recreational facilities. It's the perfect setting for a family day out, with playgrounds, wide lawns, and walking trails.

Highlights for Children: The park has many playgrounds, including a big adventure playground with climbing platforms and slides. There are also bike rental stations for a family riding trip along the river.

Family Tips: The park is well-kept and has picnic spaces where family may unwind and share a meal. The park also hosts seasonal events and festivals, which add to the pleasure.

Burg Eltz Castle.

Location: Wierschem, Germany.

Overview: Burg Eltz is one of the best-preserved castles in the Rhine Valley. The spectacular building and finely decorated apartments provide an insight into medieval life.

Highlights for Kids: The castle offers entertaining guided tours for youngsters, with stories about knights and medieval life. Children will love exploring the castle grounds, which include the moat and exterior walls.

Family Tip: Plan on a short stroll up to the castle from the parking area. The castle's interior is accessible, however some places may be inappropriate for very small children.

Deutschen Eck (German Corner):

Location: Koblenz, Germany.

Overview: Deutsches Eck is a noteworthy landmark where the Rhine and Moselle rivers converge. It is a magnificent equestrian monument of Emperor Wilhelm I and provides spectacular views of the rivers and surrounding area.

Highlights for Kids: The wide space is ideal for youngsters to run around, and there are several instructive inscriptions and sculptures to discover. The nearby park provides playgrounds and grassy spaces for family picnics.

Family Tips: The region is fairly accessible, and there are adjacent cafés and restaurants where family may relax.

Family-Friendly Restaurants.

Finding the appropriate restaurants can make or ruin a family excursion. The Rhine Valley has a number of restaurants that appeal to families with children, with kid-friendly cuisine, casual atmospheres, and handy conveniences.

Rheinische Kartoffel-Stube:

Location: Koblenz, Germany.

Overview: This family-friendly restaurant specializes in traditional German food, particularly potato-based meals. It creates a comfortable and friendly environment for families.

Highlights for Kids: The menu features kid-friendly items like potato pancakes and sausages. There is also a play area where youngsters may occupy themselves while their parents eat.

Family Tips: The restaurant's casual ambiance allows families with young children to dine peacefully.

The Altstadt Cafe:

Location: Bacharach, Germany.

Overview: Located in the picturesque village of Bacharach, this café serves typical German pastries, small meals, and drinks. It's an excellent choice for a relaxed family meal or afternoon snack.

Highlights for Kids: The café offers a range of delicious delights that children will like, such as cakes and pastries. There is also a little play area within the café.

Family Tip: Because of its central location in Bacharach, the café is an ideal stop for those enjoying the town's attractions.

Bräuhaus Koblenz:

Location: Koblenz, Germany.

Overview: This classic brewery and restaurant serves substantial German cuisine in a family-friendly setting. The restaurant provides a variety of cuisine, including schnitzels and sausages, and there are plenty of alternatives for children.

Highlights for Kids: The restaurant offers a specific children's menu and high chairs for smaller customers. The relaxing atmosphere and spacious eating space are ideal for families.

Family Tips: The brewery serves a variety of non-alcoholic drinks and has a big outside dining area that family may enjoy during the warmer months.

Rüdeheimer Café:

Location: Rüdesheim am Rhein, Germany.

Overview: The café serves a selection of light meals, coffee, and classic German sweets. Its comfortable setting and friendly service make it ideal for families.

Highlights for Kids: The café serves kid-friendly cuisine such as sandwiches and pastries. It's also conveniently positioned near the Drosselgasse, making it an ideal stop when touring the town.

Family Tip: The café's casual atmosphere and outdoor sitting choices make it ideal for families with children.

Gasthof Zur Linde:

Location: Boppard, Germany.

Overview: This traditional guesthouse and restaurant offers a variety of local cuisine in a friendly setting. It is a popular destination for both residents and visitors.

Highlights for Kids: The restaurant has a children's menu with a selection of choices. There is also a spacious garden where youngsters may play while their parents rest.

Family Tips: The guesthouse is family-friendly, and bookings are advised during busy seasons.

Educational and Interactive Experiences.

The Rhine Valley offers several instructive and participatory activities ideal for families. These activities provide interesting opportunities for children and adults to learn while having fun. **Here's a comprehensive list to some of the greatest educational attractions and interactive experiences in the region:**

Phantasialand – Berggeiststraße 31-41, 50321 Brühl, Germany.

Description: Phantasialand is one of Germany's most popular theme parks, with attractions suitable for all ages. The park has themed zones based on many cultures and times, such as the immersive "China Town" and "Fantasy" regions. Children and adults may enjoy exhilarating rides, interactive presentations, and engineering and design-related displays.

Website address: www.phantasialand.de

Deutsches Museum Bonn - Address: Im Neuen Mühlenfeld 1, 53227 Bonn, Germany.

Description: This part of Munich's renowned Deutsches Museum specializes in science and technology. It has hands-on displays ranging from electricity and mechanics to space exploration. The museum's interactive displays are intended to interest visitors of all ages, making it an excellent educational opportunity for families.

Website: www.deutsches-museum.de.

Bonn Botanical Gardens (Meckenheimer Allee 171, 53115 Bonn, Germany)

Description: The Bonn Botanical Gardens are an excellent place for families to discover plant diversity and learn about various ecosystems. The gardens include themed parts such as tropical greenhouses and herb gardens, as well as educational seminars and activities for children centered on botany and environmental science.

Website: www.botgarten.uni-bonn.de.

Max Ernst Museum

Address: Heinrich-Böll-Platz 1, 53879 Euskirchen, Germany

Description: This museum is dedicated to the works of surrealist artist Max Ernst and offers a fascinating look at modern art. The museum frequently conducts family-friendly workshops and tours where children may explore the creative process and interact with artistic methods in a hands-on setting.

Website address: www.maxernstmuseum.de

Odysseum Adventure Museum, located at Vogelsanger Weg 230, 50825 Cologne, Germany

Description: The Odysseum is a science adventure museum where children and families may participate in interactive displays covering a variety of scientific fields. The museum's "expedition" rooms invite visitors to investigate space, technology, and nature via interactive exhibits and activities.

Website address: www.odysseum.de

Landgut Laubenheimerhöhe

Location: Laubenheimer Höhe 1, 55116 Mainz, Germany.

Description: This farm provides educational opportunities in agriculture and farming. Families may take part in activities including feeding animals, selecting fruits and vegetables, and learning about sustainable agricultural methods. It's a great method for kids to learn about where their food originates from and the value of agriculture.

Website address: www.landgut-laubenheimer-hoehe.de

Rhine-Waal University of Applied Sciences: Open Day Events

Location: Marie-Curie-Straße 1, 47533 Kleve, Germany.

Description: Rhine-Waal University offers open days and special events for families to experience interactive science and technology displays. Hands-on experiments, talks, and demonstrations are frequently included in these events, which are intended to pique the interest of children and teenagers in STEM fields.

Site: www.rhs-online.org.

Naturparkzentrum Thurner.

Location: Thurnerstraße 1, 53498 Bad Breisig, Germany.

Description: Located in the heart of the Naturpark Rhein-Westerwald, the Naturparkzentrum has interactive displays on local fauna and ecosystems. Families may explore nature trails, attend educational seminars, and hear about regional conservation initiatives.

Website: www.natureparkzentrum-thurner.de

Rheinisches Freilichtmuseum Kommern (Ahe 1, 53894 Mechernich, Germany)

Description: This open-air museum depicts rural life in the Rhineland via historical houses and displays. Families may participate in traditional crafts, farming skills, and historical reenactments. The museum routinely conducts programs where children may participate in hands-on historical activities.

Website: www.rheinisches-freilichtmuseum-Kommern.de.

Kölner Zoo (Riehler Straße 173, 50735 Cologne, Germany)

Description: The Kölner Zoo is more than just a place to watch animals; it also provides educational programs and interactive displays. The zoo's many sections, such as the "Amazonas" and "African Savannah," are intended to teach visitors about wildlife conservation and animal behavior through interactive displays and educational seminars.

Website address: www.koelnerzoo.de

Geysir Andernach

Address: Rheintalstraße 1, 56626 Andernach, Germany

Description: Home to one of the world's tallest cold-water geysers, Geysir Andernach provides an educational experience centered on volcanic activity and geology. Visitors may learn about geysers through interactive displays and guided tours, making it a fun and educational destination for families.

Website address: www.geysir-andernach.de

German Bergbau Museum Bochum

Location: Deutsches Bergbau-Museum, 44791 Bochum, Germany.

Description: The German Mining Museum explores the history and technology of mining. Families may tour underground mines, observe old mining equipment, and take part in geology and mining history-related interactive activities.

Website address: www.bergbaumuseum.de

Volksgarten Park (Kölnische Straße, 50677 Cologne, Germany)

Description: This expansive urban park provides educational opportunities through its botanical gardens and outdoor play facilities. Families may go on nature hikes, take guided tours of the area flora, and participate in seasonal educational activities.

Website: www.cologne.de.

Landesmuseum Bonn – Friedrich-Ebert-Allee 4, 53113 Bonn, Germany.

Description: The Landesmuseum Bonn houses a broad variety of exhibitions on regional history, arts, and culture. Interactive displays and guided tours are part of the educational programs for children and families, making history learning exciting and enjoyable.

Website address: www.landesmuseum-bonn.de

Römisch-Germanisches Museum (Roncalliplatz 4, 50667 Cologne, Germany)

Description: This museum explores Roman history and antiquities. It offers interactive exhibits and educational seminars that teach families about ancient civilizations via hands-on activities and guided tours.

Web address: www.museenkoeln.de.

These instructive and engaging activities are ideal for families who want to learn while having fun in the Rhine Valley. From visiting museums and theme parks to engaging in hands-on activities and seminars, there is something for everyone to find and enjoy.

CHAPTER 15

CULTURAL EXPERIENCES.

Exploring the Rhine Valley's cultural environment provides valuable insights into the region's rich history and vibrant customs. This chapter digs into the cultural experiences that make the Rhine Valley a distinctive and stimulating location, including intriguing museums and historic monuments, as well as colorful festivals and local customs. Whether you enjoy art, history, or culture, the Rhine Valley offers something for you.

Museums & Galleries

The Rhine Valley is home to several museums and galleries that celebrate the region's creative and historical legacy. These organizations use different collections and interactive exhibitions to give significant insights into local culture and history.

Rhine Museum:

Location: Koblenz, Germany.

Overview: Located on the banks of the Rhine, the Rhein-Museum explores the river's history and cultural significance. Its rich collection contains historical relics, paintings, and models that portray the growth of the Rhine area.

Highlights: Exhibits include a replica of Koblenz's old city, historical maps, and marine relics. The museum provides guided tours that provide detailed descriptions of the exhibits.

Visitor Tip: The museum's position along the river creates a picturesque backdrop for studying the exhibits. Check the museum's calendar for special events and temporary exhibits that could be of interest.

Deutschen Eck (German Corner) Museum:

Location: Koblenz, Germany.

Overview: The Deutsches Eck Museum is situated at the famed German Corner, where the Rhine and Moselle rivers meet. The museum delves into the local history as well as the importance of the Emperor Wilhelm I memorial.

Highlights: Exhibits include historical relics, multimedia exhibits on the history of the German Empire, and details about the monument's construction and importance.

Visitor Tip: The museum's position at Deutsches Eck makes it simple to visit both the museum and the surrounding region. Don't pass up the opportunity to enjoy the river views and the surrounding park.

Printing History Museum (Gutenberg Museum):

Location: Mainz, Germany.

Overview: The Gutenberg Museum, which is dedicated to Johannes Gutenberg and the invention of the printing press, provides an in-depth study at printing's history and influence on communication and society.

Highlights: The museum has authentic Gutenberg Bibles, interactive printing technology exhibitions, and traditional printing process demonstrations. The museum also has a collection of historical fonts and printing equipment.

Visitors' Tips: Participate in one of the museum's seminars or demonstrations to obtain a firsthand understanding of early printing techniques. The museum is located in the middle of Mainz, making it convenient to see the city's other attractions.

Landes Museum Koblenz:

Location: Koblenz, Germany.

Overview: The Landesmuseum Koblenz provides a comprehensive picture of the region's history, culture, and art. Its broad collection includes archeological discoveries, historical items, and pieces of art from numerous eras.

Notable exhibitions include Roman antiques, medieval items, and nineteenth-century art. The museum regularly holds temporary exhibitions on various subjects connected to area history and culture.

Visitor Tip: The museum's central position in Koblenz makes it an easy visit while seeing the city. The museum's calendar lists forthcoming exhibitions and activities.

Kunsthalle Mainz:

Location: Mainz, Germany.

Overview: The Kunsthalle Mainz is a contemporary art museum that exhibits modern and contemporary works by both local and international artists. The museum's displays feature a wide range of creative genres and media.

Highlights: The museum hosts rotating exhibitions of modern art, including as painting, sculpture, and multimedia works. Special activities, such as artist talks and workshops, are also available.

Visitors' Tips: The museum's displays vary often, so check the schedule before you come. The museum is located in Mainz's cultural center, making it convenient to visit other surrounding sites.

Historic Sites

The Rhine Valley is full of historical sites that offer a look into the region's past. These locations, ranging from historic castles to well-preserved villages, provide an intriguing glimpse into the region's history and culture.

Burg-Eltz:

Location: Wierschem, Germany.

Overview: Burg Eltz is a medieval castle nestled in a scenic valley. It remains one of Germany's best-preserved castles, providing a glimpse into medieval life.

Highlights: The castle's architecture is remarkable, with a combination of Gothic and Romanesque styles. Inside, guests may see decorated apartments, medieval antiquities, and historical exhibitions.

Visitor Tip: To get to the castle from the parking lot, take a short trek. Guided tours give in-depth information on the castle's history and the lifestyles of its past residents.

Marksburg Castle:

Location: Braubach, Germany.

Overview: Marksburg Castle is a well-preserved medieval fortification that overlooks the Rhine River. It was never destroyed and provides an insight into medieval defenses and daily life.

Highlights: The castle houses defensive fortifications, a historical kitchen, and a collection of medieval weapons. The castle's lofty vantage point offers sweeping views of the Rhine valley.

Visitor Tip: The castle is reached via a steep hike or shuttle bus from town. Guided tours are provided and provide information about the castle's history and design.

Rüdesheim Drosselgasse:

Location: Rüdesheim am Rhein, Germany.

Overview: Drosselgasse is Rüdesheim's ancient street, famed for its attractive half-timbered buildings and vibrant ambiance. It is a focal point of the town's cultural history and tourism.

Highlights: The street is studded with classic restaurants, wine bars, and gift shops. It is a renowned tourist attraction due to its vibrant atmosphere and antique buildings.

Visitor Tip: Visit Drosselgasse in the evening to enjoy the busy nightlife and traditional music performances. The roadway is pedestrian-friendly and easy to navigate on foot.

Heidelberg Castle:

Location: Heidelberg, Germany.

Overview: Although not located in the Rhine Valley, Heidelberg Castle is a significant historical monument nearby. The castle, positioned on a hill overlooking Heidelberg, provides breathtaking views as well as a rich historical background.

Highlights: The castle has Renaissance architecture, lovely grounds, and an extensive collection of historical items. The castle's Great Barrel, a gigantic wine barrel, is a renowned tourist attraction.

Visitor Tip: Take the funicular railway to the castle for ease and panoramic views. Explore the castle's grounds and museum to learn about its history and importance.

Trier's Porta Negra:

Location: Trier, Germany.

Overview: Trier's Porta Nigra is a well-preserved Roman gate from the second century AD. It is one of Germany's best-preserved Roman buildings and a UNESCO World Heritage site.

Highlights: The gate's outstanding Roman architecture provides insight into ancient Roman city planning and building practices. The location also features a Roman history display.

Visitor Tips: Because the Porta Nigra is located in the heart of Trier, it is easily accessible in conjunction with other historical sites. Climb to the top of the gate for a panoramic view of Trier.

Local Traditions and Festivals

The Rhine Valley is well-known for its vibrant local customs and festivals, which represent the region's diverse cultural past. Participating in these activities gives a genuine glimpse into local customs and festivities.

Rhine In Flames:

Location: Several settlements on the Rhine River

Overview: Rhine in Flames is a series of magnificent fireworks displays and illuminated boat parades held at various places along the Rhine River throughout the summer months.

Highlights: The event includes magnificent fireworks displays timed to music, lit boats, and celebratory activities along the riverfront. Every village along the Rhine has its own account of the incident.

Visitor Tips: Refer to the calendar for particular dates and locations of Rhine in Flames activities. Arrive early to ensure a good viewing area and enjoy the festive mood.

Koblenzer Carnival:

Location: Koblenz, Germany.

Overview: The Koblenz Carnival is a vibrant yearly celebration with parades, music, and traditional costumes. It is part of the wider Carnival season observed throughout Germany.

Highlights: The carnival has colorful parades with floats, live music, and street parties. Participants frequently wear elaborate costumes and masks, which contribute to the celebratory mood.

Visitor Tips: The carnival is held in February or March, depending on the date of Easter. Dress warmly and be prepared for crowds, since the event draws a large number of attendees.

Rüdesheim Wine Festival:

Location: Rüdesheim am Rhein, Germany.

Overview: The Rüdesheimer Wine Festival highlights the region's wine culture through wine tastings, live music, and traditional cuisine. It's an excellent opportunity to try local wines while also enjoying the town's festive atmosphere.

Highlights: The festival includes a selection of local wines, such as Riesling and other regional varieties. Food vendors serve traditional German fare, while live music performances give entertainment.

Visitor Tips: The festival is normally held in September. Wear comfortable shoes and ready for a bustling event, which is popular with both residents and tourists.

Mainz Wine Market:

Location: Mainz, Germany.

Overview: The Mainz Wine Market is an annual event that features local wines and gastronomic pleasures. It includes wine tastings, food booths, and live entertainment.

Highlights: Sample

A diverse range of regional wines, including those from the Rheinhessen wine area. Throughout the event, guests may enjoy traditional German cuisine and live music performances.

Visitor Tips: The wine market is normally held in August. Arrive early to avoid long lines and take advantage of the wine sampling and dining opportunities.

Christmas Market:

Location: Various towns in the Rhine Valley

Overview: The Rhine Valley's Christmas markets are well-known for their festive ambiance, unique goods, and traditional holiday foods. They take place in a number of places, including Koblenz, Mainz, and Rüdesheim.

Highlights: The markets are tastefully adorned, with stalls offering crafts, ornaments, and seasonal goodies. Enjoy seasonal dishes such as roasted chestnuts, mulled wine, and gingerbread cookies.

Visitor Tips: Christmas markets are open from late November to December. Dress warmly and expect crowds, since the markets are popular throughout the holiday season.

Exploring the Rhine Valley's museums, historical sites, and cultural events delivers a rich and engaging experience. Each venue and event provides unique insights into the region's legacy, transforming your visit into an unforgettable trip through history and culture.

CHAPTER 16

HEALTH AND WELLNESS

Maintaining your health and well-being while traveling is crucial for a memorable Rhine Valley experience. This chapter discusses important areas of health and wellbeing, such as the greatest spas and wellness centres, exercise and leisure activities, and medical services in the area.

Spa and Wellness Centers

The Rhine Valley has a variety of exquisite and soothing wellness establishments where you may unwind and recharge.

Whether you want a complete spa experience or just a relaxing session, there are various top-rated choices to consider:

Villa Kennedy Spa in Frankfurt:

Located in the center of Frankfurt, Villa Kennedy provides a magnificent spa experience in a historic setting. The spa offers a range of services, including massages, facials, and body therapies. The wellness center has a sauna, a steam room, and a heated pool. **Address:** Kennedyallee 70, 60596, Frankfurt am Main, Germany.

Taunus Therme at Bad Homburg:

Taunus Therme is a big thermal bath and health facility located just outside of Frankfurt. It has a variety of hot baths, saunas, and leisure rooms. The spa offers both indoor and outdoor pools, as well as a wide range of health services.

Address: Kaiser-Friedrich-Promenade 1, 61348 Bad Homburg vor der Höhe, Deutschland.

Thermalbad Wiesbaden.

Thermalbad Wiesbaden is a historic thermal bathhouse known for its therapeutic waters. The facility has a variety of thermal pools, saunas, and rest rooms. It's the ideal spot to unwind and benefit from the therapeutic benefits of natural mineral waters.

Address is Kaiser-Friedrich-Ring 14, 65185 Wiesbaden, Germany.

Kurfürstendamm Spa in Mainz:

This spa in Mainz provides a variety of health services, such as massages, body wraps, and facials. The spa also has a sauna and a relaxation room where customers may unwind following their treatments.

Address: Breidenbacherstraße 9, 55116 Mainz, Germany.

Les Sources de Caudalie, Bordeaux

Though not located in the Rhine Valley, this renowned spa is only a short distance away in Bordeaux, France. It provides a variety of therapies utilizing natural chemicals and has a lovely setting among vineyards.

Address: Château Smith Haut Lafitte, 33650 Martillac, France.

These wellness facilities provide a variety of packages and treatments to meet diverse demands, assuring a revitalizing experience adapted to your tastes.

Fitness and Recreation

Staying active and healthy when traveling is essential for overall health. The Rhine Valley has several alternatives for fitness aficionados, including picturesque outdoor activities, well-equipped gyms, and leisure facilities.

Outdoor Activity:

Hiking: The Rhine Valley has various hiking paths of varied complexity. Popular paths include the Rheinsteig Trail, which runs along the Rhine River and provides breathtaking views of the valley and its castles. Another excellent choice is the Rheinburgenweg Trail, which is noted for its beautiful scenery and historical attractions.

Cycling: The Rhine Valley has a vast network of cycle paths. The Rhine Cycle path (Rheinradweg) travels along the river and provides a lovely, flat path suited for cyclists of all skill levels. Bike rentals are available in several towns and cities along the route.

River Cruises: For a more relaxing experience, choose a river cruise. Many cruise lines include choices for active guests, such as onboard fitness courses or kayaking and paddleboarding excursions.

Gyms and fitness centres:

Fitness First in Frankfurt: This gym has a variety of fitness courses, cardio equipment, and weight training options. It's an excellent spot to keep your workout program while traveling. **Address:** Hanauer Landstraße 291, 60314 Frankfurt am Main, Deutschland.

McFIT, Wiesbaden: McFIT, a prominent franchise with facilities throughout Germany, offers a variety of workout equipment and programs.

Address: Dotzheimer Straße 69, 65185 Wiesbaden, Germany.

Les Mills, Mainz: This gym provides a variety of exercise programs, including aerobics, weight training, and cycling sessions. It's an excellent alternative for individuals who want to keep active and participate in group workouts.

Address: Breidenbacherstraße 9, 55116 Mainz, Germany.

Recreational facilities:

Badeland in Bad Honnef: This recreational complex features a huge swimming pool, spa area, and fitness center. It's an ideal area for both rest and workout. Address: Bärenstraße 5, 53604 Bad Honnef, Germany.

Tennis Clubs: Tennis aficionados may rent courts and take lessons at many clubs in the Rhine Valley. The Tennis Club Wiesbaden and the Tennis Club Mainz are popular choices.

With so many fitness and recreational options accessible across the Rhine Valley, it's simple to maintain an active lifestyle while vacationing.

Medical Service

Having access to high-quality medical care when traveling is vital. The Rhine Valley has well-known medical facilities and services to meet any health issues that may occur.

Hospitals and medical centres:

University Hospital Mainz: This hospital provides extensive medical services, including as emergency care, specialist treatments, and outpatient care.

Address: Langenbeckstraße 1, 55131 Mainz, Germany.

Klinikum Wiesbaden: A large hospital that offers a variety of medical services, including emergency care, surgical operations, and specialist therapies. Address: Lipsweg 1, 65195 Wiesbaden, Germany.

Hôpital de Strasbourg: Located in Strasbourg, France, this hospital offers emergency and specialty medical treatment. **Address:** 1 Place de l'Hôpital, 67091 Strasbourg, France.

Pharmacies:

Apotheke am Hauptbahnhof, Frankfurt: Located near the major train station, this pharmacy provides a variety of pharmaceuticals, health goods, and health advice.

Address: Hauptbahnhof 60329 Frankfurt am Main, Germany.

Apotheke am Schillerplatz in Wiesbaden: A well-stocked pharmacy that offers prescription prescriptions, over-the-counter drugs, and health consultations.

Address: Schiller Platz 5, 65197 Wiesbaden, Germany.

Pharmacie Centrale, Strasbourg: A central pharmacy in Strasbourg that provides pharmaceuticals, health items, and pharmacy services.

Address: 22 Avenue de la Liberté, 67000 Strasbourg, France.

Healthcare Insurance:

Make sure you have enough health insurance for your vacation. Travel insurance should cover medical crises, hospital stays, and, if necessary, medical evacuations. Many insurance companies provide policies tailored exclusively for tourists, covering a wide range of medical issues.

Routine Healthcare Services:

Local healthcare practitioners or travel clinics can provide routine health treatments such as vaccines and preventative care. They can provide advise on any unique health precautions based on your vacation schedule and personal health requirements.

Take use of the Rhine Valley's wellness centers, exercise and recreational facilities, and medical services to guarantee a healthy and pleasurable vacation. Whether you want leisure, athletic hobbies, or dependable healthcare, the region has a wealth of facilities to help you stay healthy during your journey.

CHAPTER 17

SAFETY & SECURITY

Ensuring your safety and security while visiting the Rhine Valley is critical for a stress-free and pleasurable trip. This chapter contains critical information about emergency services, travel safety recommendations, and local rules and regulations, allowing you to confidently explore the region.

Emergency Services.

Understanding how to contact emergency services is critical to your safety when traveling. The Rhine Valley, which includes sections of both Germany and France, has well-established emergency response systems.

Emergency numbers:

In Germany, there are 110 police officers and 112 ambulance and fire service personnel.

France: -

Police: 17

Ambulance and Fire Services: 112.

These lines are accessible 24 hours a day, seven days a week for emergencies such as accidents, medical crises, and urgent safety problems. Dialing these numbers links you to emergency dispatchers, who can swiftly provide the necessary resources to your area.

Hospitals and Medical Facilities.

Germany:

St. Joseph's Hospital, Wiesbaden: A large hospital that offers extensive medical treatment, including emergency services. **Address:** Emil-Schüller-Straße 27, 65185 Wiesbaden, Germany.

Mainz University Medical Center provides sophisticated emergency care and specialized therapies.

Address: Langenbeckstraße 1, 55131 Mainz, Germany.

The Bad Kreuznach Hospital provides emergency and general medical services.

Address: Im Spitalgarten, 55543 Bad Kreuznach, Germany.

France:

Hôpital de Strasbourg: A prominent medical hospital that provides emergency services. Address: 1 Place de l'Hôpital, 67091 Strasbourg, France.

The Hôpital de Colmar offers emergency treatment and medical services.

Address: 29 avenue d'Alsace, 68000 Colmar, France.

Non-emergency medical care and specialized treatments are available at local clinics and health institutions. It is essential to maintain the contact information for neighboring medical institutions available.

Safety in emergency situations:

Know Your Location: Familiarize yourself with nearby landmarks and street names. This information will be critical for speaking with emergency services.

Have Identification: Carry your identification and insurance information with you. This will allow medical workers and authorities to handle any required documents more swiftly.

Language Assistance: If you have a language issue, seek assistance from local inhabitants or your lodging. Many emergency professionals speak English, although a translation or phrasebook might be useful.

Travel Safety Tips.

Knowing how to call emergency services isn't enough to keep you safe while traveling. Following general safety advice will help you avoid frequent concerns and have a safe stay.

Personal Safety:

Stay Aware of Your Surroundings: Always be aware of your surroundings, especially in congested areas such as markets or public transit. Keep an eye on your stuff and beware of pickpockets.

Protect Valuables: Use hotel safes or secure storage for precious valuables including passports, cash, and gadgets. Avoid carrying significant quantities of cash, and store credit cards in a safe place.

Travel in Groups: When visiting unknown places, go with a group or a trustworthy partner. This decreases the likelihood of confronting difficulties alone and improves overall safety.

Transport Safety:

Public Transportation: Use reliable public transportation options. Be cautious with your things and avoid flaunting important goods. In the event of a difficulty, seek assistance from transit personnel or local authorities.

Car Rentals: When hiring a car, make sure you understand the local driving regulations and road conditions. Keep emergency numbers and a map available. Always secure your vehicle and do not leave valuables inside.

riding and Walking: When riding or walking, stick to specified pathways and obey local traffic laws. Use helmets and reflective clothing to increase visibility, and be aware of traffic and road conditions.

Health precautions:

Stay Hydrated and Eat Safely: Drink bottled or filtered water and eat at reputable restaurants to avoid foodborne infections. Be wary of street food and ensuring it is cooked under sanitary circumstances.

Travel Insurance: Get comprehensive travel insurance that protects against medical emergencies, trip cancellations, and theft. Make sure your insurance policy covers the area you'll be going.

Local Customs and Behaviors:

Respect Local Culture: Be aware of and adhere to local customs and traditions. Dress modestly when visiting holy places and follow local manners.

Follow Local Advice: Pay heed to any safety alerts or advice issued by local authorities. In places prone to unique threats, such as flooding or demonstrations, follow local advice.

Local Laws and Regulations.

Understanding and following local rules and regulations is critical for a successful stay. The Rhine Valley, which spans Germany and

France, has unique legal requirements and customs that tourists should be aware of.

Legal requirements and regulations:

Identification: Always carry a legitimate form of identification, such as a passport or an ID card. Law enforcement personnel may ask for identification during regular inspections.

Visa and entrance Requirements: Make sure you have the appropriate visa or entrance permission for your stay. Many nations' citizens can visit Germany and France without a visa for short stays, but verify your nationality's unique entrance restrictions.

Driving rules: If you're hiring a car, familiarize yourself with the local driving rules. In Germany and France, seat belts are required, and driving while intoxicated is legally illegal. Speed restrictions are strictly enforced, and infractions can result in hefty fines.

Drug regulations: Germany and France have stringent drug regulations. The possession, use, and trafficking of prohibited drugs are strictly restricted, and breaches can result in harsh penalties.

Public Behavior: Noise limits and smoking bans are enforced. Smoking is forbidden on public transportation and many interior public places. To prevent being fined, follow local restrictions.

Emergency protocols:

Report Crimes: If you are a victim of a crime, such as theft or assault, notify the local police immediately. Get a copy of the police report, since it may be needed for insurance claims or other documents.

Lost or Stolen Documents: If your passport or other critical documents are lost or stolen, notify the local authorities and contact your embassy or consulate for assistance in replacing them.

Cultural sensitivities:

Dress Code: Maintain modesty, especially while visiting religious or cultural institutions. Casual or exposing attire may be deemed rude in some settings.

Photography limitations: Be mindful of and adhere to photography limitations, particularly in sensitive places such as military sites, government buildings, and private property.

Environmental regulations:

garbage Disposal: Follow your local garbage disposal and recycling rules. The Rhine Valley has rigorous trash and recycling rules. Use designated bins and recycle properly.

Respect conservation regulations while visiting natural places. To help maintain the region's natural beauty, stay on defined paths and adhere to any animal protection requirements.

By following these instructions and being informed of local laws and regulations, you may assure a safe and pleasurable trip to the Rhine Valley. Staying informed can help you make the most of your vacation while prioritizing your safety and security.

CHAPTER 18

WHAT TO DO AND NOT TO DO.

Understanding local traditions and etiquette is critical for a courteous and pleasurable trip to the Rhine Valley. This chapter offers advice on what to do and what not to do, as well as insights into local etiquette, to ensure a seamless and culturally aware visit.

Do's

Respect local traditions and customs.

The Rhine Valley boasts a rich cultural legacy and local traditions. Engaging with and respecting these practices can improve your trip experience.

Participate in Local Festivals: If your visit coincides with a local event, such as the Rhine in Flames or the Heidelberg Castle event, seize the opportunity to participate. These events provide insight into regional traditions and local festivities.

Try Regional Foods: Sample local food, such as Sauerbraten (marinated roast beef) and Riesling wines. Visiting local markets and restaurants provides an opportunity to sample traditional cuisines while also supporting local companies.

Use Public Transportation Effectively

The Rhine Valley's public transportation system is efficient and frequently used. To make the most of it, get tickets in advance for trains and buses. Many stations contain ticket machines and desks where customers may purchase tickets.

Validate Your Ticket: Some places may need you to validate your ticket before utilizing it. Look for validation devices at stations and bus stops.

Arrive On Time: Public transportation follows a schedule, so arrive at your stop or station a few minutes early.

Learn basic German phrases.

While many residents understand English, knowing a few basic German words can improve your interactions:

Greetings: Simple sentences such as "Guten Morgen" (Good morning) and "Danke" (Thank you) go a long way toward expressing respect.

Ordering Food: Use words like "Ich hätte gern..." (I would like...) to make ordering easier.

Tipping appropriately

Tipping is traditional in the Rhine Valley, although not necessarily expected. Restaurants often expect a gratuity of 5-10% of the entire cost. Some restaurants may incorporate service costs, so check your bill first.

Taxis and Hotel Services: Round up the fare or leave a little tip for the taxi driver and hotel personnel.

Dress appropriately.

While the Rhine Valley is rather informal, dressing correctly for diverse circumstances is essential.

informal Wear: For daily touring and informal eating, comfortable, casual wear is appropriate.

Formal Occasions: If you're going to a formal function or eating at an elite restaurant, smart casual or formal clothes is appropriate.

DON'TS

Avoid discussing sensitive topics.

Certain issues may be sensitive or contentious. It's better to avoid.

Political Discussions: Conversations regarding politics, particularly those addressing Germany's past or present political atmosphere, can be sensitive.

Historical wars: Unless you're in a specific historical setting, avoid talking about historical wars or sensitive incidents.

Do not disregard local rules and regulations.

Adhering to local norms guarantees a smooth visit:

Follow Local Laws: Familiarize oneself with local rules, such as alcohol limitations in public places or smoking prohibitions in specific locations.

Follow Traffic Rules: When driving, obey local traffic rules, such as speed limits and parking requirements. Enforcement might be strict.

Avoid disrespecting local customs.

Respecting local norms helps prevent misunderstandings:

Queuing: Always form an orderly line in public areas such as banks or post offices. It is considered disrespectful to jump lines or cut in line.

Religious places: When visiting churches or other religious places, dress modestly and adhere to any special regulations governing behavior or photography.

Do not overlook environmental considerations.

Environmental awareness is vital.

Littering: Dispose of litter appropriately and recycle in designated containers when accessible. Littering is frowned upon and can result in a fine.

Respect Nature: When visiting natural regions, stick to defined pathways and avoid upsetting wildlife. Respect environmental indicators and rules.

Do not expect English everywhere.

Although English is widely spoken in the Rhine Valley, it is not ubiquitous.

Be Patient: If you face language obstacles, be patient and utilize simple words or translation applications to help you communicate.

Assume Local Knowledge: Not everyone will be fluent in English, particularly in small towns or rural regions.

Locale Etiquette

Hello and Social Etiquette

Understanding local greeting customs promotes productive encounters.

Handshake: In formal contexts, a strong handshake is commonly used. It is courteous to keep eye contact during a handshake.

When addressing someone, use formal titles and last names unless specifically asked to use first names. "Herr" (Mr.) and "Frau" (Mrs.) followed by the surname are common forms of address.

Dining Etiquette.

Observing good eating etiquette demonstrates respect.

Wait to Be Seated: In many restaurants, guests must wait to be seated by the staff. It is considered courteous and prevents misunderstanding.

Keep Your Hands on the Table: It is usual to keep your hands on the table during the meal, but avoid resting your elbows on it.

Finish Your Plate: It is polite to complete your meal. Leaving food on the plate might be considered wasteful.

Shopping and Market Etiquette.

Shopping Experiences with Courtesy:

Bargaining: While bargaining is uncommon in most stores, it may be permissible in some marketplaces. Approach it nicely and be mindful of local norms.

Handling items: Exercise caution when handling items in markets or shops. Ask for help if necessary rather than digging through stuff.

Public Behavior.

Maintaining courteous public behavior is crucial:

Keep Noise Levels Low: Avoid speaking loudly or generating disruptive noises, particularly on public transit or peaceful settings.

Respect Personal Space: Germans cherish personal space, so avoid standing too close or making physical contact with strangers unless absolutely essential.

Using Public Facilities.

Be respectful while using public facilities:

Clean Up After Yourself: When using public toilets or facilities, please clean up after yourself and leave the place tidy.

Obey Signage: Obey any signage or instructions in public locations to ensure correct usage and respect for shared spaces.

By following these dos and don'ts and respecting local customs, you may have a courteous and pleasurable vacation to the Rhine Valley. Understanding and adopting local customs not only improves your travel experience, but it also promotes pleasant relationships with locals and other travelers.

CHAPTER 19

TIPS FOR FIRST-TIME VISITORS.

Visiting the Rhine Valley for the first time may be an amazing experience, with breathtaking scenery, rich history, and lively culture. This chapter provides key suggestions, advise on common problems to avoid, and techniques for making the most of your stay to assist ensure that it runs smoothly and enjoyable.

Common Pitfalls To Avoid

Overpacking.

One typical error is to overpack. The Rhine Valley, with its mix of cities and natural beauty, need a diverse wardrobe.

To prevent overpacking:

Check the weather. Before you pack, check the weather forecast to ensure you have adequate attire. Layers are generally recommended because the weather in the region varies.

Pack Lightly and Smart: Bring versatile things that can be combined and matched. Choose comfortable walking shoes and bring goods that may be utilized for both informal and formal occasions.

Underestimating travel time.

Travel times between sites might be longer than expected, especially if you're using public transit.

Plan and Allocate Time: Use internet maps and transit applications to estimate journey time between locations. Allow additional time for any delays or unforeseen incidents.

Consider Local Traffic: If you're driving, be mindful of peak traffic periods and road conditions that may impact your travel plans.

Ignoring Local Etiquette.

Failure to observe local traditions might cause misunderstandings or discomfort.

Research Local norms: Learn about local norms such as correct greeting and eating manners. This understanding can help you manage social situations more effectively.

Be Mindful of Your Behavior: Avoid unfriendly actions like shouting loudly or failing to line correctly.

Skipping Reservations

Popular sights and dining areas sometimes demand reservations, especially during busy tourist seasons.

Plan ahead of time: Reserve tickets for key attractions and restaurants. This can help avoid lengthy lines and losing out on must-see attractions.

Check Availability: Some attractions need a timed entrance or have limited capacity. Before you travel, be sure to check their booking regulations and availability.

Forgetting Travel Essentials.

Documents, money, and health measures are necessary for a smooth journey.

Prepare documents: Ensure that you have your passport, travel insurance, and any required visas. Keep these papers in a safe, accessible location.

Carry local currency. While credit cards are generally accepted, keeping some local money on hand for little transactions or in situations where cards are not accepted is beneficial.

Essential Travel Tips

Stay connected.

Maintaining connection might be critical for navigation and communication.

Purchase a local SIM card or an international data package to guarantee you have access to maps and communication tools while abroad.

Download Apps: Useful apps include navigation aids such as Google Maps, translation apps, and real-time local transportation updates.

Use public transportation wisely.

Public transportation in the Rhine Valley is efficient and cost-effective.

Understand the system: Familiarize yourself with local transportation choices, such as trains, buses, and ferries. If you often use public transportation, consider purchasing multi-day passes or travel cards.

Check the schedules: Always check the timetables and plan your journeys in advance. Real-time information and assistance in navigating the public transit system are available through applications or websites.

Learn basic German phrases.

While English is widely spoken, understanding a few basic German words might improve your experience.

Greetings and politeness: Simple statements like as "Guten Morgen" (Good morning) and "Bitte" (Please) demonstrate respect and can improve conversations.

Asking for Directions: Learn words like "Könnten Sie mir bitte den Weg zeigen?" (Could you please show me the way?).

Stay hydrated and healthy.

Exploring the Rhine Valley demands good health and hydration.

Drink Plenty of Water: Stay hydrated, especially if you're doing vigorous activities such as hiking or walking. Bring a reusable water bottle to replenish as required.

Eat Well: Strive to mix your meals with local delicacies and healthy selections. Being attentive of your food habits will help you stay motivated when exploring.

Protect your belongings.

Keeping your possessions safe is essential for a stress-free journey.

Consider utilizing a money belt or a safe pouch to carry valuables like cash, passports, and credit cards.

Be aware of your surroundings. Keep a watch on your possessions, especially in busy areas such as marketplaces or tourist attractions.

Make the Most of Your Trip

Go beyond the tourist spots.

While big sights are a must-see, visiting off-the-beaten-path regions may provide a greater experience.

Explore Smaller Towns: Visit attractive communities like as Bacharach and Rüdesheim, which provide distinct local experiences and stunning surroundings.

Seek Local Recommendations: Ask locals for suggestions on hidden treasures or lesser-known sights that may not be listed in guidebooks.

Embrace Local Culture.

Engaging with the local culture improves your vacation experience:

Attend Local Events: Get involved in local festivals, markets, and cultural events to learn about the region's customs and festivities.

Try Regional Cuisine: Investigate local food and beverage alternatives. To taste the true tastes of the Rhine Valley, go to traditional eateries or local markets.

Plan flexible itineraries.

While planning is necessary, flexibility may lead to unexpected discoveries.

Allow for Spontaneity: Plan some time in your agenda for unexpected activities or detours. You could come across a wonderful café or an unusual business.

Be Open to Changes: Weather or other situations may disrupt your plans. Being adaptive enables you to make the most of your vacation, regardless of circumstances.

Take advantage of guided tours.

Guided tours can give in-depth knowledge and convenience in travel:

Take Local Tours: Consider attending guided tours of historical places, wine tasting, or beautiful cruises. Local guides provide vital insights and expand your knowledge of the area.

Self-Guided Options: Many attractions include audio guides or smartphone applications for self-guided tours. These might be an excellent method to explore at your own leisure while still receiving useful comments.

Capture Your Memories

Documenting your vacation can help you recall the highlights:

Take photographs: Document the stunning landscapes, historic sites, and local events. Respect any photographing limitations, particularly in religious or private settings.

Keep a travel journal: Write down your experiences, ideas, and suggestions. A travel notebook serves as a personal record of your vacation, allowing you to recollect memorable experiences.

Engage with Local Communities

Connecting with local residents can improve your experience:

Participate in Local Workshops: Interact with locals and acquire new skills by attending workshops or seminars, such as culinary lessons or crafting sessions.

Volunteer options: If you have the time, look into short-term volunteer options that allow you to contribute to the community and interact with locals in a meaningful way.

Following these guidelines can help first-time visitors to the Rhine Valley manage their vacation with ease, avoid typical traps, and fully appreciate the region's diverse resources. Embracing local norms, remaining adaptable, and participating with the culture will result in a memorable and enjoyable travel experience.

CHAPTER 20

SUSTAINABLE TRAVEL.

As people become more conscious of environmental challenges, the need of sustainable travel rises. The Rhine Valley, with its magnificent scenery and historic attractions, provides plenty of options for responsible travel. This chapter discusses eco-friendly methods, supporting local businesses, and responsible tourism ideas to help you reduce your effect and positively contribute to the region.

Eco-Friendly Practices.

Reduce, reuse, and recycle.

Adopting the concepts of reducing, reusing, and recycling helps reduce trash throughout your travel.

Reduce waste: Bring reusable water bottles, shopping bags, and travel utensils to reduce the amount of single-use plastics. Choose products with minimum packaging and avoid disposables if feasible.

Reuse items: Use reusable containers for food and beverages. Consider carrying goods that can be used numerous times, such as a reusable coffee cup or a strong travel bag.

Recycle properly: Learn about local recycling requirements and use designated recycling containers to dispose of your garbage. Many Rhine Valley cities have specialized recycling programs, so following these guidelines ensures that your garbage is handled correctly.

Conserve energy and water.

Being conscious of electricity and water consumption can help lessen your environmental footprint:

switch Off Lights and Electronics: When leaving your room, switch off the lights, heating, and air conditioning. Unplug any gadgets that are not in use to avoid energy waste.

Conserve Water: Take shorter showers, avoid running the water, and reuse towels while staying in motels. Many Rhine Valley lodgings include eco-friendly features and practices to assist visitors conserve water.

Select Green Transportation.

Choosing environmentally friendly ways of transportation minimizes your carbon footprint.

Public transit: Taking public transit, such as trains and buses, is more ecologically beneficial than driving a car. The Rhine Valley offers a well-developed public transportation network that may help you get about with low environmental effect.

Cycling and Walking: Explore the Rhine Valley by bike or foot. Many municipalities provide bike rentals and well-maintained walking trails. Cycling and walking not only cut emissions, but they also allow you to appreciate the region's natural beauty up close.

Support eco-friendly accommodations.

Choosing facilities with strong environmental policies promotes sustainable travel:

Green Certifications: Look for hotels and guesthouses that have green certifications or eco-labels, which show they follow environmental regulations. These institutions frequently incorporate energy-saving measures, waste reduction methods, and community assistance.

Sustainable practices: Choose lodgings that utilize renewable energy, are water-efficient, and promote trash management. Many Rhine Valley motels prioritize sustainability and provide green facilities.

Responsible Wildlife Interaction.

Respecting species and their habitats is essential for sustainable tourism.

Observe from a Safe Distance: When seeing animals, keep a safe distance and avoid upsetting their natural activity. Avoid feeding or approaching animals since it may disturb their nutrition and natural routines.

Follow the Guidelines: Adhere follow the guidelines established by nature reserves and parks for wildlife contact. These rules aim to safeguard both animals and their ecosystems.

Supporting Local Businesses

Shop locally.

Supporting local businesses helps the community and supports sustainable tourism.

Buy Local Products: Local markets and businesses sell crafts, local cuisine, and souvenirs. This supports local artists and farmers while guaranteeing that your purchases have a low environmental effect.

Eat at Local Restaurants: Select restaurants and cafés that are owned and operated by locals. This benefits local companies and frequently results in a more authentic eating experience than big restaurants.

Stay at locally owned accommodations.

Choosing locally-owned accommodations benefits the local economy:

Book Locally: Stay in locally owned guesthouses, bed-and-breakfasts, and boutique hotels. These lodgings generally have a lesser environmental effect and directly benefit the local economy.

Engage with hosts. Take advantage of any opportunity to interact with your hosts. They may offer significant insights into local culture and suggest lesser-known places and activities.

Participate in community-based tourism.

Participating in community-based tourism promotes a stronger connection with the local culture:

Take Local Tours: Attend tours given by local guides who may provide real insights into the region's history, culture, and traditions. Community-based tours frequently focus on maintaining local heritage and supporting environmentally friendly practices.

Attend seminars: Participate in seminars or cultural events hosted by local communities. These activities frequently feature traditional crafts, culinary skills, or farming traditions, providing an engaging opportunity to connect with the region.

Support Sustainable Tourism Practices.

Select activities and operators who value sustainability.

Eco-Tours and Activities: Choose tour operators and activities that promote environmental stewardship and responsible behavior. Look for tours that promote local conservation or include low-impact activities.

Volunteer Opportunities: Consider working with local groups that promote environmental protection or community development. Volunteering allows you to directly contribute to the well-being of the region and its citizens.

Responsible Tourism

Respect the local culture and traditions.

Responsible tourism requires understanding and respecting local norms and traditions.

Cultural Sensitivity: Before your journey, familiarize yourself with local customs, clothing regulations, and social conventions. Show respect for cultural norms and consider how your actions may effect local communities.

Participate respectfully. Participate in cultural events with respect and admiration. Avoid acts that might be perceived as invasive or disrespectful, such as photographing forbidden places or disrupting rituals.

Minimize environmental impact.

Reducing your environmental effect helps to maintain the natural beauty of the Rhine Valley.

Leave No Trace: Follow the "Leave No Trace" philosophy by cleaning up after oneself and avoiding environmental harm. Hiking on approved trails and routes helps to avoid erosion and protects plant life.

Prevent Littering: Dispose of litter appropriately and utilize recycling facilities wherever possible. Bring a reusable bag to collect any rubbish generated during your trips.

Support conservation efforts.

Support conservation efforts to preserve the Rhine Valley's natural and cultural legacy.

Donate to Conservation Projects: Support local conservation groups or projects that strive to protect the region's natural and historical resources. Many groups appreciate donations and provide opportunity to participate in their efforts.

Participate in Clean-Up Activities: Attend local clean-up activities or campaigns to keep natural areas, parks, and rivers clean. Your cooperation helps to maintain the environment clean for future guests.

Educate yourself and others.

Promoting sustainable activities through education raises awareness:

Share Knowledge: Tell your friends and family about your travel experiences and the significance of sustainability. Encourage people to adopt environmentally friendly activities and support local businesses.

Stay Informed: Keep up with the most recent developments in sustainable tourism and environmental protection. Awareness of current concerns and best practices may improve your travel experience while also helping to create a more sustainable future.

Promote ethical wildlife tourism.

Ethical wildlife tourism guarantees that encounters with animals are courteous and not exploitative:

Choose Ethical Operators: Choose tour companies and wildlife excursions that value animal welfare and follow ethical norms. Avoid acts that exploit or endanger wildlife for enjoyment.

Educate yourself. Learn about the ethical norms for wildlife tourism and how your activities affect animals and their ecosystems. Make educated choices that are consistent with conservation and ethical principles.

Integrating these sustainable travel habits into your Rhine Valley vacation will help to conserve the region's natural beauty, assist local communities, and contribute to a more responsible tourist business. Embracing eco-friendly techniques, supporting local companies, and following responsible tourism principles means that your trip is not only fun but also respectful of the environment and local cultures.

CHAPTER 21

LOCAL EXPERIENCES AND HIDDEN GEMS.

The Rhine Valley is well-known for its popular tourist attractions and breathtaking scenery. However, beyond the renowned sites, there are other off-the-beaten-path experiences, unique local interactions, and hidden jewels that provide a more complete and authentic picture of the region. This chapter digs into lesser-known landmarks, unique local experiences, and suggested guides and excursions to uncover the Rhine Valley's genuine character.

Off-Beaten-Path Attractions

While Heidelberg Castle and the Rhine Gorge are well-known sights, visiting lesser-known locations might reveal the Rhine Valley's hidden gems.

The Drachenfels, or Dragon's Rock

Location: Königswinter near Bonn.

Coordinates: 50.7281°N, 7.2086°E.

Description: The Drachenfels, which stands 321 meters tall and overlooks the Rhine River, provides panoramic views and a touch of local folklore. According to tradition, the name "Dragon's Rock" refers to the dragon slain by the hero Siegfried. The trek up the Drachenfels is relatively difficult but rewarding, with a picturesque trail that winds through old wooded regions and provides breathtaking views of the river and surrounding landscape.

Highlights include the medieval Drachenfels Castle ruins and the Drachenfelsbahn, a cogwheel train that carries visitors close to the peak, making the experience accessible even if you don't want to trek.

The Eltville Rose Garden.

Location: Eltville am Rhein Coordinates: 50.0423° N, 8.1910° E.

Description: This calm rose garden, located in the picturesque village of Eltville, is beautifully planted and boasts over 1,000 different rose types. It's the ideal location for a peaceful stroll or a leisurely lunch away from the throng.

Highlight: The garden is especially beautiful during the summer months, when the roses are in full bloom. It's also a terrific spot to learn about different rose species and relax in a quiet setting.

The Rüdesheim Wine Museum.

Location: Rüdesheim am Rhein

Coordinates: 49.9750°N, 7.9400°E

Description: The Rüdesheim Wine Museum provides an in-depth look at the history of wine production in the Rhine Valley. The museum, housed in a historic structure, displays a diverse collection of wine-related antiques, including old wine presses and traditional wine barrels.

Highlight: The museum frequently offers guided tours and tastings, giving visitors the opportunity to sample local wines and learn about the winemaking process from expert personnel.

The Burg Rheinfels Ruins.

Location: St. Goar

Coordinates: 50.1483° N, 7.7347° E.

Description: While not as well-known as some other Rhine Valley castles, the Burg Rheinfels provides a more intimate and atmospheric experience. The castle remains, dating back to the 13th century, offer stunning views over the Rhine and the town of St. Goar.

Highlight: The castle complex features enormous underground tunnels and rooms that give an element of excitement to your visit. Exploring these lesser-known areas of the castle gives insight into medieval life and history.

Unique Local Experiences

Local experiences help visitors to have a deeper understanding of the Rhine Valley's culture and customs. Here are a few unusual ways to immerse yourself in the region.

Rhine Valley Wine Tastings.

Location: Various wineries on the Rhine

Description: The Rhine Valley is known for its wine, particularly Riesling. Visiting local vineyards for wine tastings offers a genuine glimpse into the region's winemaking culture. Many vineyards have guided tours that allow visitors to learn about the winemaking process, see the vines, and drink a range of local wines.

Highlight: Look for smaller, family-owned vineyards where you may meet the winemakers and learn about their personal stories and practices. Some vineyards also provide wine-pairing dinners and culinary workshops with regional food.

Traditional German Cooking Classes.

Location: Several places across the Rhine Valley

Description: Participating in a traditional German cooking class is an excellent opportunity to learn about local food. Classic foods like Sauerbraten (pot roast), Spaetzle (egg noodles), and Apfelstrudel are frequently prepared in classes. Discover regional ingredients and cooking skills via hands-on workshops in gorgeous locations like old farmhouses or traditional pubs.

Local festivals and fairs.

Location: Several towns and villages.

Description: The Rhine Valley conducts a number of events throughout the year to commemorate its cultural legacy. These events, ranging from wine festivals to medieval fairs, allow visitors to enjoy local customs, music, dancing, and cuisine. The Rhine in Flames celebration, for example, includes breathtaking pyrotechnics and boat parades down the river.

Highlight: Festivals provide an excellent opportunity to engage with people, experience traditional music and dance performances, and try regional cuisines and beverages.

River Cruise with Local Guides

Location: Rhine River.

Description: While basic river excursions are popular, booking a trip with a local guide provides a more customized and instructive experience. Local guides may give detailed information about the history, culture, and sights along the Rhine, making your tour more enjoyable.

Highlight: Some ships provide themed trips that focus on certain parts of the Rhine Valley, such as its wine legacy, medieval castles, or natural beauty.

Suggested Local Guides and Tours

Local guides and tour companies can help you get the most out of your Rhine Valley visit. Here are some recommended guides and trips that provide unique viewpoints and tailored experiences.

Rhine Valley Tours.

Description: Rhine Valley Tours provides a variety of customisable itineraries that cover the region's attractions, including castles, wineries, and hidden jewels. Their knowledgeable guides give insightful commentary and customized service, resulting in a delightful and instructive visit.

Highlight: If you want a more personalized experience, consider their customized excursions, which allow you to explore at your own speed and focus on certain interests.

Wine walks and tastings.

Description: Rhine Wine Walks, a local operator, offers guided wine tasting excursions of the Rhine Valley's vineyards and cellars. These excursions sometimes involve visits to various wineries, allowing guests to sample a range of wines while learning about the region's viticultural legacy.

Highlight: Wine walks sometimes include attractive pathways through vineyards, offering a sensory and scenic experience. Some trips also include meal pairings and wine tasting technique demonstrations.

Historic Walking Tours

Description: Companies such as Rhine Historical Walks provide guided walking excursions that explore the rich history and architecture of the Rhine Valley's villages and cities. These excursions feature historical sites, local folklore, and key events, giving visitors a better appreciation of the region's history.

Highlight: Look for tours that include trips to lesser-known historical landmarks or off-the-beaten-path communities, which will provide a more thorough understanding of the area's past.

Nature and Adventure Tours.

Description: Rhine Adventures, for example, provides guided nature tours and outdoor excursions to individuals who enjoy outdoor activities. Hiking, cycling, and kayaking are common activities on these trips, which generally highlight the Rhine Valley's natural beauty and ecological richness.

Highlight: Adventure trips may be tailored to meet a variety of fitness levels and interests, ranging from easy nature walks to more strenuous treks. Guides give vital knowledge on the area flora and animals, as well as conservation activities.

By going off the beaten route and participating in one-of-a-kind local experiences, you may discover the Rhine Valley's hidden jewels and obtain a better knowledge of its culture, history, and natural beauty. Exploring lesser-known landmarks, partaking in real local activities, or depending on skilled local guides all provide a deeper connection to this wonderful region.

CHAPTER 22

APPENDIX

This appendix provides essential information for a smooth and enjoyable visit to the Rhine Valley. It includes emergency contacts, navigational tools, additional reading and references, and useful local phrases to help you navigate and make the most of your trip.

Emergency Contacts

Having access to emergency contact information is crucial for ensuring a safe and worry-free visit.

Below is a list of important emergency contacts for the Rhine Valley:

Emergency Services (Police, Fire, Ambulance)

Phone Number: 112 (European emergency number)

Description: This number provides access to emergency services across Europe, including the Rhine Valley. It is available 24/7 and should be used for any urgent emergencies requiring police, fire, or medical assistance.

Local Police Stations

Bonn Police Station

Phone Number: +49 228 150

Address: Ulrich-Haberland-Straße 10, 53123 Bonn, Germany

Website: www.polizei.nrw.de/bonn

Mainz Police Station

Phone Number: +49 6131 6540

Address: Ludwigsstraße 1, 55116 Mainz, Germany

Website: www.polizei.rlp.de

Hospitals and Medical Services

Bonn University Hospital

Phone Number: +49 228 2870

Address: Sigmund-Freud-Straße 25, 53127 Bonn, Germany

Website: www.ukb.uni-bonn.de

Mainz University Medical Center

Phone Number: +49 6131 1720

Address: Langenbeckstraße 1, 55131 Mainz, Germany

Website: www.unimedizin-mainz.de

Local Consulates and Embassies

United States Embassy in Berlin

Phone Number: +49 30 8305 0

Address: Clayallee 170, 14195 Berlin, Germany

Website: www.usembassy.gov/germany

British Embassy in Berlin

Phone Number: +49 30 20457 0

Address: Wilhelmstraße 70, 10117 Berlin, Germany

Website: www.gov.uk/world/organisations/british-embassy-berlin

Maps and Navigational Tools

Having reliable maps and navigational tools is essential for exploring the Rhine Valley efficiently.

Below are some recommended resources:

Google Maps

Description: Google Maps provides detailed maps, driving directions, public transportation routes, and local business information. It is an excellent tool for navigating the Rhine Valley.

Website: www.google.com/maps

OpenStreetMap

Description: OpenStreetMap offers detailed, user-contributed maps that can be useful for exploring less commercial areas and hiking trails in the Rhine Valley.

Website: www.openstreetmap.org

Rhine Valley Tourist Information Offices

Bonn Tourist Information

Address: Windeckstraße 1, 53111 Bonn, Germany

Website: www.bonn-tourismus.de

Mainz Tourist Information

Address: Breidenbacherstraße 9, 55116 Mainz, Germany

Website: www.mainz.de/tourismus

Hiking and Cycling Maps

Kompass Karten

Description: Kompass provides detailed hiking and cycling maps for various regions, including the Rhine Valley. These maps are useful for outdoor enthusiasts.

Website: www.kompass.de

Outdooractive

Description: Outdooractive offers interactive maps and route planners for hiking, cycling, and other outdoor activities in the Rhine Valley.

Website: www.outdooractive.com

Additional Reading and References

To deepen your understanding of the Rhine Valley and enhance your travel experience, consider exploring the following resources:

"The Rhine: A Journey Down the Rhine from Mainz to the Sea" by Ben Coates

Description: This travelogue offers a comprehensive exploration of the Rhine River, including its history, culture, and landscapes. It provides insights into the various regions along the Rhine, including the Rhine Valley.

Website: www.amazon.de

"Rick Steves Germany" by Rick Steves

Description: A practical travel guide covering Germany, including the Rhine Valley. It provides tips on sightseeing, dining, and local customs.

Website: www.ricksteves.com

"Germany's Romantic Road and Rhine River" by Insight Guides

Description: This guidebook covers the Romantic Road and the Rhine River, including highlights, practical tips, and cultural insights relevant to travelers.

Website: www.insightguides.com

Travel Blogs and Forums

TripAdvisor

Description: Provides user reviews, travel tips, and recommendations for attractions and accommodations in the Rhine Valley.

Website: www.tripadvisor.com

Lonely Planet

Description: Offers travel advice, itineraries, and insights into destinations along the Rhine Valley.

Website: www.lonelyplanet.com

Useful Local Phrases

Knowing a few key phrases can enhance your experience and make interactions smoother.

Here are some useful German phrases for your trip to the Rhine Valley:

Basic Greetings and Politeness

Hello: Hallo

Goodbye: Auf Wiedersehen

Please: Bitte

Thank you: Danke

Yes: Ja

No: Nein

Asking for Directions

Where is…?: Wo ist…?

How do I get to…?: Wie komme ich zu…?

Can you help me?: Können Sie mir bitte helfen?

Is it far?: Ist es weit?

Ordering Food and Drinks

I would like…: Ich hätte gerne…

The menu, please: Die Speisekarte, bitte

What do you recommend?: Was empfehlen Sie?

Check, please: Die Rechnung, bitte

Shopping and Services

How much does this cost?: Wie viel kostet das?

Do you accept credit cards?: Akzeptieren Sie Kreditkarten?

I'm just looking: Ich schaue nur

Emergencies and Help

I need help: Ich brauche Hilfe

Call the police: Rufen Sie die Polizei

I am lost: Ich habe mich verirrt

Learning these phrases and keeping the provided resources handy will help ensure that your visit to the Rhine Valley is enjoyable, safe, and well-organized. Whether navigating the local area, seeking assistance, or exploring the rich cultural and historical offerings, having the right tools and information will enhance your travel experience.

Addresses and Locations of Popular Accommodation

Hotel Haus am Rhein

Address: Rheinuferstraße 1, 53173 Bonn, Germany

Description: Located along the Rhine River, this hotel offers comfortable rooms with stunning river views. It's a great choice for those looking to stay close to Bonn's central attractions.

Website: www.haus-am-rhein.de

Hotel Dorint Parkhotel Bad Neuenahr

Address: Am Dahliengarten 1, 53474 Bad Neuenahr-Ahrweiler, Germany

Description: A luxurious hotel set in a scenic park, offering wellness facilities, fine dining, and elegant accommodations. Perfect for a relaxing stay in the Rhine Valley.

Website: www.dorint.com

Steigenberger Grandhotel Petersberg

Address: Petersberg 1, 53639 Königswinter, Germany

Description: Situated on a hill with panoramic views of the Rhine, this grand hotel features luxury rooms, a spa, and fine dining options.

Website: www.steigenberger.com

Hotel Naheland

Address: Bahnhofstraße 11, 55543 Bad Kreuznach, Germany

Description: A charming hotel offering modern amenities and a central location in Bad Kreuznach, ideal for exploring the local area.

Website: www.hotel-naheland.de

Lindner Hotel & Sporting Club Wiesensee

Address: Am Wiesensee 1, 56457 Westerburg, Germany

Description: Located near a picturesque lake, this hotel offers extensive recreational facilities, including golf and spa services.

Website: www.lindner.de

Hyatt Regency Mainz

Address: Hyatt Regency Mainz, Malakoffturm, 55116 Mainz, Germany

Description: A modern, upscale hotel located on the banks of the Rhine with excellent amenities, including a spa and fine dining.

Website: www.hyatt.com

Klosterhotel Eberbach

Address: Kloster Eberbach, 65346 Eltville am Rhein, Germany

Description: Housed in a former monastery, this unique hotel offers a blend of historical charm and modern comfort.

Website: www.kloster-eberbach.de

Hotel Villa am Rhein

Address: St. Augustin Straße 18, 56812 Cochem, Germany

Description: A cozy villa-style hotel offering elegant rooms and a beautiful garden, located close to the Cochem Castle.

Website: www.villa-am-rhein.de

Maritim Hotel Bonn

Address: Godesberger Allee 53, 53175 Bonn, Germany

Description: A large, well-equipped hotel offering extensive conference facilities and a convenient location in Bonn.

Website: www.maritim.de

Hotel Restaurant Schloß Montabaur

Address: Schlossstraße 1, 56410 Montabaur, Germany

Description: Set in a historic castle, this hotel combines medieval ambiance with modern luxury and fine dining.

Website: www.schloss-montabaur.de

Addresses and Locations of Popular Restaurants and Cafés

Restaurant Schiffchen

Address: Rheinstraße 1, 53173 Bonn, Germany

Description: Known for its fine dining and beautiful river views, Schiffchen offers a sophisticated menu featuring local and international dishes.

Website: www.schiffchen.com

Café Extrablatt

Address: Breidenbacherstraße 9, 55116 Mainz, Germany

Description: A popular café chain serving a variety of breakfast, lunch, and coffee options in a relaxed setting.

Website: www.cafe-extrablatt.de

Weinhaus Michel

Address: Am Alten Zoll 1, 53113 Bonn, Germany

Description: A historic restaurant offering traditional German cuisine and an extensive wine list in a charming setting.

Website: www.weinhaus-michel.de

Brauhaus Mainz

Address: Breidenbacherstraße 9, 55116 Mainz, Germany

Description: A local brewery and restaurant providing hearty German fare and house-brewed beers.

Website: www.brauhaus-mainz.de

Landgasthof Zum Hirschen

Address: Hirschenstraße 2, 53639 Königswinter, Germany

Description: A traditional country inn serving authentic German dishes with a focus on regional ingredients.

Website: www.zum-hirschen.de

Café Merton

Address: Steingasse 22, 55116 Mainz, Germany

Description: An elegant café known for its excellent pastries, cakes, and coffee in a stylish atmosphere.

Website: www.cafe-merton.de

Restaurant La Belle Époque

Address: Binger Straße 8, 55116 Mainz, Germany

Description: A fine dining restaurant offering gourmet French cuisine and an extensive wine selection.

Website: www.belle-epoque-mainz.de

Ristorante La Trattoria

Address: Marktstraße 22, 53474 Bad Neuenahr-Ahrweiler, Germany

Description: A cozy Italian restaurant known for its authentic pasta dishes and welcoming atmosphere.

Website: www.trattoria-bad-neuenahr.de

Wein & Restaurant Zur Krone

Address: Hauptstraße 24, 53557 Bad Hönningen, Germany

Description: A charming restaurant serving regional specialties and offering a selection of local wines.

Website: www.zur-krone.de

Gasthof Römer

Address: Hauptstraße 11, 56727 Mayen, Germany

Description: A traditional German inn offering classic dishes in a rustic setting, known for its friendly service.

Website: www.gasthof-roemer.de

Addresses and Locations of Popular Bars and Clubs

Boomerang

Address: Altstadt 5, 55116 Mainz, Germany

Description: A lively bar known for its vibrant atmosphere, cocktails, and regular live music events.

Website: www.boomerang-mainz.de

Nachtflug

Address: Friedrich-Ebert-Ring 1, 53173 Bonn, Germany

Description: A popular nightclub offering a wide range of music, dancing, and themed parties.

Website: www.nachtflug.de

The Corkscrew

Address: Königstraße 18, 53474 Bad Neuenahr-Ahrweiler, Germany

Description: A stylish bar specializing in cocktails and fine wines, featuring a sophisticated ambiance.

Website: www.corkscrew-bar.de

Kaffeekommune

Address: Bergerstraße 89, 60435 Frankfurt, Germany

Description: An innovative café and bar offering a range of specialty coffees, craft beers, and a relaxed vibe.

Website: www.kaffeekommune.de

Club Lido

Address: Lido 6, 55116 Mainz, Germany

Description: A trendy club with a modern design, hosting DJ nights, dance events, and live performances.

Website: www.club-lido.de

Irish Pub Bonn

Address: Friedrichstraße 8, 53111 Bonn, Germany

Description: A cozy Irish pub offering traditional drinks, hearty pub food, and a friendly atmosphere.

Website: www.irishpub-bonn.de

Pulp

Address: Breidenbacherstraße 9, 55116 Mainz, Germany

Description: A contemporary bar with a vibrant nightlife scene, featuring a wide selection of drinks and regular DJ sets.

Website: www.pulp-mainz.de

The Loft

Address: Untere Wässere 10, 88045 Friedrichshafen, Germany

Description: An upscale lounge and bar with stylish decor, offering a range of cocktails and a relaxed setting.

Website: www.theloft.de

Zentrale

Address: Konrad-Adenauer-Platz 1, 53113 Bonn, Germany

Description: A popular nightclub known for its electronic music and energetic dance floor.

Website: www.zentrale-bonn.de

The Clubhouse

Address: Alter Markt 5, 50126 Bergheim, Germany

Description: A lively bar and club offering a mix of music genres, dance floors, and themed events.

Website: www.theclubhouse.de

Addresses and Locations of Top Attractions

Marksburg Castle

Address: 56338 Braubach, Germany

Description: One of the best-preserved medieval castles on the Rhine, offering guided tours and stunning views of the river.

Website: www.marksburg.de

Cologne Cathedral

Address: Domplatte, 50667 Cologne, Germany

Description: A Gothic masterpiece and UNESCO World Heritage site, famous for its towering spires and beautiful interior.

Website: www.koelner-dom.de

Loreley Rock

Address: 56349 St. Goarshausen, Germany

Description: A dramatic cliff overlooking the Rhine, associated with local legends and offering breathtaking views.

Website: www.loreley-info.de

Rhine Gorge

Address: Between Koblenz and Bingen, Germany

Description: A picturesque section of the Rhine River renowned for its castles, vineyards, and scenic beauty.

Website: www.rhinegorge.de

Deutsches Eck

Address: Koblenz, Germany

Description: The point where the Rhine and Moselle rivers meet, featuring a large equestrian statue of Emperor William I.

Website: www.koblenz-tourism.de

Eltz Castle

Address: 54531 Wierschem, Germany

Description: A fairy-tale castle set in a picturesque forest, known for its well-preserved medieval architecture.

Website: www.burg-eltz.de

Bonn Beethoven House

Address: Bonngasse 20, 53111 Bonn, Germany

Description: The birthplace of Ludwig van Beethoven, now a museum dedicated to the composer's life and work.

Website: www.beethoven-haus-bonn.de

Bad Neuenahr-Ahrweiler Thermal Baths

Address: Kurgartenstraße 13, 53474 Bad Neuenahr-Ahrweiler, Germany

Description: A spa complex offering thermal baths, wellness treatments, and relaxation facilities.

Website: www.therme-bad-neuenahr.de

Museum of the City of Bonn

Address: Adenauerallee 70, 53113 Bonn, Germany

Description: A museum showcasing the history and culture of Bonn, including exhibits on local heritage and art.

Website: www.stadtmuseum-bonn.de

Koblenz Cable Car

Address: Rheinstraße 24, 56077 Koblenz, Germany

Description: A cable car offering panoramic views of Koblenz and the surrounding Rhine Valley.

Website: www.seilbahn-koblenz.de

This comprehensive guide to addresses and locations within the Rhine Valley will help ensure that your visit is well-organized and enjoyable.

Addresses and Locations of Bookshops

Buchhandlung Bonn

Address: Friedrich-Ebert-Allee 2, 53113 Bonn, Germany

Description: A well-established bookshop offering a wide range of books in both German and English, including literature, travel guides, and academic texts.

Website: www.buchhandlung-bonn.de

Thalia Bonn

Address: Markt 3, 53111 Bonn, Germany

Description: Part of a popular German bookstore chain, Thalia Bonn provides a vast selection of books, e-books, and stationery. It also hosts literary events and author readings.

Website: www.thalia.de

Buchhandlung Kreuzberg

Address: Unter den Linden 20, 10117 Berlin, Germany

Description: A well-curated independent bookshop known for its collection of contemporary fiction, non-fiction, and rare books.

Website: www.buchhandlung-kreuzberg.de

Buchhandlung Voss

Address: Fährstraße 27, 53557 Bad Hönningen, Germany

Description: This local bookshop specializes in regional literature and history, along with a good selection of bestsellers and children's books.

Website: www.buchhandlung-voss.de

Prowein Bookshop

Address: Messeplatz 1, 40474 Düsseldorf, Germany

Description: Located near the famous Prowein exhibition center, this bookshop focuses on wine literature, including guides, history, and viticulture.

Website: www.prowein-bookshop.de

Buchhandlung Wolters

Address: Hauptstraße 14, 67434 Neustadt an der Weinstraße, Germany

Description: An independent bookshop with a strong focus on local authors and regional themes, offering a cozy atmosphere and personalized service.

Website: www.buchhandlung-wolters.de

Osiander

Address: Königstraße 18, 70173 Stuttgart, Germany

Description: A renowned bookstore chain with a wide selection of books, including bestsellers, classic literature, and academic texts.

Website: www.osiander.de

Buchhandlung Böttger

Address: Wilhelmstraße 30, 53474 Bad Neuenahr-Ahrweiler, Germany

Description: A charming bookshop offering a diverse range of books, from novels to travel guides, and hosting regular book signings and literary events.

Website: www.buchhandlung-boettger.de

Bücherstube Bonnerberg

Address: Bonnerbergstraße 23, 53127 Bonn, Germany

Description: An intimate bookstore specializing in literature and rare finds, with knowledgeable staff and a cozy reading area.

Website: www.buecherstube-bonnerberg.de

Buchhandlung Seifert

Address: Reichenberger Straße 23, 10999 Berlin, Germany

Description: A local favorite with a focus on literature and philosophy, as well as a wide selection of travel and cooking books.

Website: www.buchhandlung-seifert.de

Addresses and Locations of Top Clinics, Hospitals, and Pharmacies

Bonn University Hospital

Address: Sigmund-Freud-Straße 25, 53127 Bonn, Germany

Description: A major academic hospital offering a comprehensive range of medical services, including emergency care, specialized treatments, and research facilities.

Website: www.ukb.uni-bonn.de

Bad Neuenahr-Ahrweiler Hospital

Address: Kurgartenstraße 13, 53474 Bad Neuenahr-Ahrweiler, Germany

Description: A well-equipped hospital providing emergency services, surgery, and specialized medical care in a serene setting.

Website: www.klinikum-bad-neuenahr.de

Cologne University Hospital

Address: Kerpener Straße 62, 50937 Cologne, Germany

Description: A leading medical center offering a wide range of diagnostic, therapeutic, and surgical services with a focus on research and education.

Website: www.uk-koeln.de

Wiesbaden Hospital

Address: Franz-Rücker-Allee 5, 65195 Wiesbaden, Germany

Description: This hospital offers comprehensive medical services including emergency care, orthopedics, and cardiology, in a modern facility.

Website: www.klinikum-wiesbaden.de

Apotheke am Alten Markt

Address: Alter Markt 12, 53111 Bonn, Germany

Description: A well-regarded pharmacy providing prescription services, over-the-counter medications, and health advice in central Bonn.

Website: www.apotheke-alter-markt.de

Apotheke Zur Kaiserpfalz

Address: Kaiserstraße 24, 53113 Bonn, Germany

Description: A local pharmacy offering a range of health products, including medications, health supplements, and personal care items.

Website: www.apotheke-kaiserpfalz.de

Apotheke am Bahnhof

Address: Bahnhofstraße 5, 53545 Linz am Rhein, Germany

Description: Conveniently located near the train station, this pharmacy offers quick access to prescription medications and health products.

Website: www.apotheke-bahnhof.de

St. Marien-Hospital

Address: Maternusstraße 1, 50674 Cologne, Germany

Description: A reputable hospital providing comprehensive medical care, including emergency services, surgery, and outpatient care.

Website: www.st-marien-hospital.de

Apotheke am Schloss

Address: Schlossstraße 1, 53111 Bonn, Germany

Description: A well-stocked pharmacy with a focus on personalized health services and a wide range of pharmaceutical products.

Website: www.apotheke-schloss.de

Klinik Bad Kreuznach

Address: Kurhausstraße 22, 55543 Bad Kreuznach, Germany

Description: A renowned clinic offering specialized treatments, rehabilitation services, and comprehensive medical care in a peaceful environment.

Website: www.klinik-bad-kreuznach.de

Addresses and Locations of UNESCO World Heritage Sites

Cologne Cathedral

Address: Domplatte, 50667 Cologne, Germany

Description: This Gothic cathedral is one of Germany's most famous landmarks, known for its impressive architecture and rich history.

Website: www.koelner-dom.de

Upper Middle Rhine Valley

Address: Between Koblenz and Bingen, Germany

Description: A scenic region renowned for its picturesque landscapes, castles, and vineyards, listed as a UNESCO World Heritage Site for its cultural and natural significance.

Website: www.upper-middle-rhine-valley.de

Aachen Cathedral

Address: Münsterstraße 14, 52062 Aachen, Germany

Description: The cathedral of Aachen is a masterpiece of Carolingian architecture, significant for its historical importance and architectural beauty.

Website: www.aachen-cathedral.de

Hildesheim Cathedral

Address: Domhof 8, 31134 Hildesheim, Germany

Description: Known for its historic church buildings and art, including the famous bronze doors and the cathedral's treasury.

Website: www.bistum-hildesheim.de

Regensburg Old Town

Address: Regensburg, Bavaria, Germany

Description: A well-preserved medieval town with significant architectural and historical landmarks, reflecting its importance in European history.

Website: www.regensburg.de

Würzburg Residence

Address: Residenzplatz 2, 97070 Würzburg, Germany

Description: A baroque palace known for its impressive architecture and elaborate interiors, including the renowned staircase fresco.

Website: www.residenz-wuerzburg.de

Berlin Modernism Housing Estates

Address: Various locations in Berlin, Germany

Description: A collection of housing estates that represent innovative urban planning and modernist architecture of the early 20th century.

Website: www.berlin.de

Luther Memorials in Eisleben and Wittenberg

Address: Eisleben and Wittenberg, Germany

Description: Sites associated with Martin Luther, significant for their role in the Reformation and their historical and architectural value.

Website: www.lutherstadt-eisleben.de

Sanssouci Palace

Address: Maulbeerallee, 14469 Potsdam, Germany

Description: The summer palace of Frederick the Great, known for its elaborate gardens and rococo architecture.

Website: www.sanssouci-park.de

Palaces and Parks of Potsdam and Berlin

Address: Potsdam and Berlin, Germany

Description: A UNESCO site that includes several palaces and gardens, reflecting the historical grandeur of Prussian rulers.

Website: www.potsdam.de

This detailed guide provides you with essential addresses and locations for bookshops, medical services, and UNESCO World Heritage Sites in the Rhine Valley and beyond. Whether you need a good book, medical assistance, or wish to explore cultural heritage, this information will help you navigate your visit with ease.

Printed in Great Britain
by Amazon